DISC

From Nashv

Praise for *Punching Holes in the Dark*

"Robert Benson writes in a voice at once tender and warm, an old-friend voice, the sort that seeps so easily into your heart. He's given us—in words emphatically whispered—a holy mantra, a charge, a sacred instruction: "Punch holes in the darkness." Yet, he offers, too, the promise: "The Light will come." And, finally, the lasting exhortation: "Be the Light." This often darkening world needs Robert Benson and his light-seeking charge." —**Barbara Mahany**, author of *Slowing Time*

"Today's world is filled with darkness—both within and without. But what are we going to do about it? Reading the exquisite words of Robert Benson might be just the catalyst one needs in order to muster the courage for punching holes in the dark. With eloquent vulnerability, Benson reveals his own deep struggle to reconcile the Christ-follower's mandate to bring Light to the world with how we all too often stumble and fail in the process. But he leaves us with bright visions of possibility and stories calling us to notice the sacred among the ordinary. I suspect you might read this book at least twice and then, if you're like me, endeavor to do the following: 'Where there is Light, we are to celebrate. Where there is darkness, we are to raise our fist and punch a hole in it—as hard as we can, as often as we can.'" —**Lucinda Secrest McDowell**, author of *Dwelling Places*, blogger at EncouragingWords.net

"God is everywhere. Sometimes, however, our eyes are blinded by pain and loss and confusion. Robert Benson helps us open them. His words leap from the page into the heart, helping us discover and discern God's eternal presence and wisdom." —**Rabbi Evan Moffic**, author of *What Every Christian Needs to Know About the Jewishness of Jesus* and *What Every Christian Needs to Know About Passover*

"This book is beautiful. The words and the message. Benson has given us a gift with *Punching Holes in the Dark*. Those wrestling with darker times in their own lives or those grieving the darkness of violence, poverty, fear, and hatred in our world will be reminded that darkness does not win in the end, that we are not in perpetual night, but that the light of dawn can and does and will break through. This is the kind of book that you share with everyone in your life. They and you will be blessed." —**The Reverend Chaz Howard**, PhD, author of *Pond River Ocean Rain* and University Chaplain of the University of Pennsylvania

Praise for Robert Benson's Previous Works

"It is a great irony that all of us who love Jesus and know that he prays for us, even now, that we 'may all be one,' have such a difficult time loving one another. Robert Benson doesn't exactly tell us how to do it, but he does tell an honest story about the ways that Jesus' prayer is getting worked out in his own life." —**Eugene Peterson**, Professor Emeritus, Regent College, author of over thirty books, including the Gold Medallion Award winner *The Message: The Bible in Contemporary Language*

"In looking at his own life with candor and hope, Robert Benson helps us to look at our own. His words have the ring of truth." —**Frederick Buechner**, finalist for the Pulitzer Prize, author of *A Long Day's Dying*, *The Sacred Journey*, *Now and Then*, *Telling Secrets*, and *The Eyes of the Heart*

"The work instilled in me an awe that has been lacking in my relationship with God. And a deep desire for liturgy that has been dormant for decades. I'm sure this was meant to be a book one savors over days, but I inhaled it all at once." —**Liz Curtis Higgs**, author of more than thirty books, with more than 4.5 million copies in print

"For such a teacher as this, all the Church should be grateful." —**Phyllis Tickle**

"Benson's writing is spare, simple, understated, always faintly humorous, and very forceful without seeming to be. He writes cleanly and honestly. He writes lovingly, yet never with sentimentality. He writes helpfully, yet never with a secret agenda of telling us 'how to.'" —**Paula D'Arcy**, author of *Song for Sarah*, *The Divine Spark*, and *Gift of the Red Bird*

Continued on page 151

ROBERT BENSON

Punching Holes in the Dark

LIVING
IN THE
Light of the
World

Abingdon Press
Nashville

PUNCHING HOLES IN THE DARK
LIVING IN THE LIGHT OF THE WORLD

Copyright © 2016 by Robert Benson

Macro Editor: Ramona Richards

Library of Congress Cataloging-in-Publication Data has been requested.

ISBN 13: 978-1-4267-4958-2

16 17 18 19 20 21 22 23 24 25—10 9 8 7 6 5 4 3 2 1

MANUFACTURED IN THE UNITED STATES OF AMERICA

This book is for Phyllis Tickle,
good friend of my house and dear friend to my scribblings.

It is for Dale and Robbins and Johnny,
who reminded me of things I already knew.

It is for all those who take friend Champ's advice
to keep punching holes in the darkness.

And, as always, it is for the Friends of Silence & of the Poor,
whoever & wherever you may be.

Contents

And that light is the Light of the world,
and the darkness will never overcome it.

The Gospel

Grant us such an awareness of your mercies, we pray,
that with truly thankful hearts we may show forth our praise,
not only with our lips but with our lives.

The Prayers of the People

There is a crack in everything,
that's how the light gets in.

Leonard Cohen

A First Thing

In the beginning was the Word.

The Gospel

Our Father who art in heaven,
may your kingdom come upon us and cleanse us.

The Prayers of the People

Shout the gospel from the rooftops. If necessary, use words.

Attributed to Saint Francis of Assisi

Y ou're religious, aren't you?" she said.
Evidently I proclaimed the gospel once, for about twenty minutes, without saying any of the words I had been taught in Sunday school.

I have lived as a churchman all my life.

One might even say I started out as a church boy. My father was a preacher. The first bunk beds I remember my brother and I sharing were in the back of the church my father pastored when I was young. He and my mother slept in the room next door.

Years of performing in a Christian rock-and-roll band in churches, years of working in a Christian music company whose audience was the crowd of people who already believed in the things we were saying, years of making books largely aimed at the people who base their lives on the same theological pillars I do hardly count as going forth into all the world. It was not so much spreading the gospel as securing the gospel, not so much spreading seeds as it was saving the gospel from harm from those folks out there who did not hold the Story dear in the way we did.

There is some possibility that when I was a schoolboy, the most overtly evangelistic thing I did was have one of those silver and red One Way stickers on the rear window of my Volkswagen. Looking back, I have come to understand I pasted it there not so those who did not believe might see it but so others like me would know I belonged to the correct tribe. When the kingdom finally came, I wanted to be certain I was in that number even if I was double-parked.

I never proclaimed the gospel much at all to those who did not already believe it. I generally made sure to proclaim the gospel safely within the confines of the church walls where everybody in the room already held the belief that Jesus was the Messiah and their personal Savior to boot. We had a good time, but we were hardly carrying the gospel to the ends of the earth.

I think a lot lately about the sense many of us have that we cannot see much evidence of the kingdom that is already here.

We do not, and cannot, by definition, know much about the kingdom to come. But the One Who Came Among Us not only came to reassure us of the gift of the kingdom that is yet unseen but to proclaim the presence of the kingdom already among us, even when we cannot see it and we cannot hear it.

"It is within you and it is without you," He said, "and you do not even see it," which suggests the One Who Made Us reigned over all of us even before He came to live among us.

Even for those of us who believe in it, long for it, and keep ourselves busy proclaiming it to each other, the kingdom that is already here is evidently easy to miss.

I read the papers each day.

I read the reports of wars both great and small. I read where again today there were bombings of the fathers and mothers and sons and daughters of someone somewhere, and I long for peace. I would settle for truce most days, or even an informal cessation of hostilities.

I read the stories of random and not-really-random violence and am stunned by what we are capable of doing to each other, what we do to each other in the name of everything from greed to God.

I listen to the world around me each day. I listen as the general tone of discourse about anything of value and anyone who matters—and who is different and therefore does not matter—grows less and less civil, less and less reasonable, less and less hopeful.

I listen as the ones who would lead us discount and mislead and disregard us, all of us, once we have voted them into their places of authority. I listen to their bickering and blustering as the societies we inhabit become more and more dysfunctional, and as the very planet we live on comes apart at its very seams.

Every day I wonder if today there will be a single thoughtful conversation about the things that matter in the halls of power and media and religion.

I look around me each day. I look with dismay, knowing that we who have much might not do much at all on this day for those who only have a little. I watch as we do not feed those who are hungry, protect those who are vulnerable, insure those who are at risk, provide for those who are sick, and care for those who are desperate.

I look at what our treasure seems to be after all is said and done each day and where we spent our treasure and who we spent our resources on.

I look around, and I long for us to make any sacrifice at all for someone else, be the sacrifice reasonable or lively or otherwise.

I walk the streets of the city where I live most every day. I walk past the houses of the old, the ones who are alone and afraid and hungry, the ones who hide behind their curtains and their locked doors so no one will know. I go past the ones who have no doors to lock and no roof over their heads either, the ones who sleep in the streets where I walk. I go past young people with blank faces and sullen eyes and angry hearts and I wonder what will become of them.

I long for the streets themselves to be empty of fear of all kinds.

I have come now to carry a kind of darkness around with me everywhere, within me and without me.

It is not the same darkness the One Who Made Us gave to us each night for the refreshment of our minds and bodies, as it is called in the old prayer book, the darkness given for silence and rest, gifts we now squander with abandon.

Rather, I carry with me some portion of our self-made darkness each day. I can no longer pretend that such darkness is not also all around us and among us and within us.

I read the Ancient Story, and I make my prayers. I walk the aisles of holy spaces. I listen to my own heart, and I look for signs and wonders. I carry my share of our darkness, and I long for the Light.

"Darkness is not dark to You; the night is as bright as the day; darkness and light to You are both alike," writes the psalmist. The darkness may not be dark to the One Who Made Us, but there are days when it is very dark to me.

Each morning before the sun comes, I sit in the remains of the comforting dark given to us for our rest. And I wait for the world to begin again. I wait for the kingdom, the one that is already here.

I was in the advertising business at the time I was accused of being religious. Advertising is not exactly a ministry, I confess.

The nature of my work in those days required I maintain working relationships with several of the local media outlets on behalf of my clients. She was the ad rep for a newspaper. Several of my clients were in her pages each month, and I was regularly treated to a free lunch. To those who would suggest there is no free lunch in the world, I would say it depends on your career choice. Advertising will get you free lunches, as will being a writer.

We were talking about the ad buys for an upcoming campaign when she accused me of being religious.

"Well, yes," I said, taken aback. Actually I was taken to whatever three steps past aback is called.

"I knew it," she said. "I could tell by the way you move through the world with joy and hope and humor and kindness." I did not smile to myself then because I had not yet heard his famous words, but there is reason to suspect St. Francis would have smiled in my direction for at least a single moment.

If that moment was the high point of my "go forth and preach the gospel" days, then I will take the applause of St. Francis and be grateful. Who knows, it may happen again some fine day.

Being around church folks all my life, I know some of us are terribly discouraged because we see few signs of the kingdom that is already here in the days in which we live in the hope of the other kingdom, the one we have been told is to come. We who have been honestly and powerfully and hopefully proclaiming the gospel sometimes see no signs of Light at all. Our discouragement can become deep enough we even stop looking for the kingdom that has already come and spend our days only longing for the kingdom that will come some day to put us out of what we all too often come to see as our misery.

In the beginning was the Word and the Word became flesh and dwelt among us and told us, oh, by the way, the kingdom is already here. How do we who call ourselves by the Holy Name—we, of all people—keep missing the kingdom all around us?

Born Again, Again

To all who believed the good news,
He gave the power to become the children of Light.

The Gospel

Grant that we may find you and be found by you.

The Prayers of the People

Keep punching holes in the darkness.

Champ Traylor

*I*t is spring, and I am at home in one of my birthplaces.

Nearly twenty-five years ago I first came to this place, an old Methodist campground in what passes for mountains in northern Alabama—almost forty years old at the time, more broken than I ever expected I might be in my life, and even more broken than I knew at the time. People I did not know took me in here and became my friends.

When I was here the first time, I was led into, stumbled into, wandered into, fell into everything my life as a writer and as a person was to be about for the rest of my days. Over the course of two years, coming and going every ninety days as was the rule of the community, I was born again here in these rooms, on these fields, in these woods.

To say I was born again in those days is an understatement.

This is the place where I learned about the art of the liturgy and the practice of the ancient ways of prayer and wisdom, of drawing on the treasures of the ones who went before us. It is where I learned to make a friend and to keep one through the years and miles and heartaches and changes. It is where I first sat in a circle and learned to tell my truth to another. ("Death by sharing," is the way I first thought of it.)

Now I sit in the circle again. A different circle now, as I am one of those who teaches or speaks or whatever is the proper way to describe what writers do when they are not writing and are asked to come and be what they call a presenter. The best I can ever do is to be present.

Among the people I face when I stand up each day at the appointed time are those who are being born again. It is holy ground, and my hope is that I will not get in the way. "The job's impossible," wrote Clive Barnes about his art and craft, "and one must pray that one will be only moderately incompetent." Amen, so be it.

It is evening and our day's work is done. The folks who are the leaders for this week gather up for yet another round of death by sharing. We have said our prayers and taught the classes and managed the logistics and put out the fires that broke out behind the scenes. We are all spent and tired.

One of my first friends from those long-ago days is sitting in the circle. He, too, has been asked to come and speak. In fact, he and I are often asked to come and speak to the next crowd of folks who come to the Academy. He and I laugh about the notion of it. That we might someday be asked to help run the asylum for a few days never entered our minds all those years ago.

When we were first here, we thought we were sitting at the feet of wise and wonderful people. We were stunned by what we heard them say, and our lives were changed forever in a hundred little ways. To be asked to be one of those people now makes us both giggle. Neither of us can believe we are on the program.

The cartoonist Gary Larson once said his life of paper-and-ink drawing and humor seemed so improbable he began to live in constant fear that one day there would be a knock at his door, and he would answer the knock to see two men in black FBI suits. "There has been a terrible mistake," they would say to him. "Here is your shovel."

My friend and I feel the same way whenever we think about our being adjunct faculty for these events.

"So, Robert, how is your journey these days?" The standard opening question for a round of death by sharing.

I have a split second to make a choice.

On the one hand, I can say the things I know they would like to hear me say. "My life is good, my work is going well. Everyone at my house is generally happy, joyous, and free, generally blessed beyond measure in our art and our home and our spiritual life." Are those not the things an adjunct faculty member should say? After all, according to the promotional literature, the invitation was extended to me because of my rich wisdom and deep piety and balanced life. As a former advertising copywriter, I have some sense about the truth behind the copy that is written on anything.

On the other hand.

On the other hand, I am discouraged on the evening they ask this question, discouraged enough I can barely breathe.

Some of my discouragement is purely personal.

The recent recognition of yet another chronic disease with which I will have to contend for the rest of my life, the financial struggles attendant to a household choosing a life in the pursuit of art rather than the pursuit of wealth, the being suddenly uninvited to participate in the work and life of the parish I have loved and served for some twenty years, the kindhearted, gently delivered rejection of a manuscript I love as much if not more than any I have written—all these things weigh upon me that evening as the question came round.

Some of my discouragement was based in the life of the world in which we live. The list was, and is still, very long—people organizing up to make sure some do not have access to health care, prospects of more war to try and clean up the mess from the last ill-advised one, patent ignoring of the fact we are ruining the planet for which the One Who Made Us appointed us as stewards, political maneuvers designed to make sure people not like us have no voice, poverty in the gap between the wealthy and the poor in the largest economy in the world, the widespread notion that more guns is the solution to the killing of one hundred of us each day by someone who can buy as many guns as he likes. The fact the charges into the dark are often led by those who call themselves followers of the Christ was almost more than I could bear.

A dark place is the only way to describe the place where I was that evening, emotionally spent, tired of being tired of the same things. A place where the ongoing search for the presence of the Light among us seemed fruitless and useless.

The weight I was feeling in the dark that evening in the mountains of northern Alabama was larger than me and my house and my neighborhood. As ridiculous as I sound when I say it—please note I try to stay ahead of everyone in calling myself ridiculous. After all these years, I have learned it is best to go ahead and acknowledge my ridiculousness, others take note very quickly, and they may not be as gentle with me as I need for them to be—as ridiculous as it might sound, I was feeling the weight of a large portion of what passes for the civilized world and the part of the world for which I pray for something akin to civilized to break out.

For me to say I pray for the Light is absolutely the case. For me to say I see the Light each day is absolutely presumptuous.

On that evening, I found myself thinking, yet again, that if the kingdom has already come, for the life of me, I have not lately caught a glimpse.

My old friend looked at me with the same sweet grin with which he has always held me, and so I opted for the truth. If you cannot tell the truth at home, then where are you going to do so?

I regard myself as a wordsmith, and I generally try never to blurt. But I could not help myself.

I complained bitterly about what I perceived as the failure of the Church to respond to several important issues of our times.

I ranted about our collective culpability in nonsensical wars, political struggles that hurt people instead of help, and our quickness to divide and exclude rather than welcome and include. I criticized our leaders, from the pulpit to the parish, from the city council to the Congress, from the evangelical to the orthodox.

It was honest and quiet, as I seldom raise my voice. But it was awful. Even as I voiced my hopelessness, I was painfully aware of my helplessness.

My friends simply listened to me. Bless them, they are better men than me. One of them was wise, one of them was gentle, one of them opened a window for me that will change the way I see the world for the rest of my life. I went into our time together an angry, disappointed, discouraged man. I came out very different.

"All that came to be was alive with this Life. This Light shines in the darkness, and the Darkness will never overcome it."

I hear my three friends saying to me there is a very real possibility I will never notice the Light of the kingdom that is already here if I spend all of my time looking at the Dark all around us.

The One Who Came said the same thing to the religious folks to whom He first spoke. "The kingdom does come at some future time and place, it is already here. It is within you and it is without you and it is all around you, and you do not see it and you do not hear it."

The kingdom is not confined to those rooms where we gather up to worship and practice our piety and devotion. It is everywhere and we do not see, He is saying, saying to them and saying to me and to you, if anyone is listening.

Perhaps we are not looking. Perhaps we are so aware of the Dark we do not see the Light.

One of my father's dearest friends was a man named Champion. His mother, in a fit of hope or longing, gave him the name. His friends have always called him Champ.

Champ lived in the same house with my folks when they were all at seminary in Kansas City. I have no memory of his being there, but evidently he babysat my brother and me while our dad went to classes and our mother went to work. He still takes credit for teaching me to ride a tricycle.

Champ is a larger-than-life character—raconteur, writer, preacher, professor, theologian, pundit—a person who commands a room whenever he walks into one. Of all of the good friends my father had over the years, and he had many of them, Champ is likely the only one who qualifies as an intellectual.

I talked to him the other day on the telephone for the first time in years. His voice was exactly the same as I have always remembered. Based on my age alone, he must be 112 years old by now, but you cannot tell it by his mind or his passion or his voice. Just thinking about him makes me smile.

I ended up with a fair number of my father's letters after he passed away. Many of them are from Champ. Just holding the old onion-skin paper with the typos and the white-out makes me grin and weep with joy.

He very often closed his letters with this phrase: "Keep punching holes in the darkness, my friend."

I have begun to say to myself that perhaps that is how the Light of the world sneaks in.

As I sat with my friends talking about the dark and the Light that night, with Champ's voice ringing in my ears, I began to stumble upon two very important things.

One was that my friends evidently love me enough to listen to me, hear me, and hold me close in spite of me. Champ's voice alone reminded me of the way that friends can love each other over the years and of the gift of such love.

The other was this: The Light *is* in the world. The kingdom has already come. My not seeing it is not a function of the Light not being here among us, it is a function of my insistence upon only looking at the dark.

People I know, people I do not know, people I will meet someday, people I will never know, people down the pew from me, people across the street—untold numbers of them—are all punching holes in the darkness.

And the Light of the world is sneaking in.

"Starting now," a favorite sung phrase from an Ingrid Michaelson song I listen to a lot these days—poets are found everywhere, if you look and listen—starting now, I will spend my days and hours and minutes looking for the Light of the world.

I'll not be a happy idiot who is not aware of the Dark around us. But the Darkness will never overcome us, we who keep punching holes in the darkness.

"Let there be light," we say at the prayers to begin the day, "and there is light. And God saw that the Light was good. This very day, the Lord has acted."

And starting now, I plan to no longer miss the Light because I look only at the Dark.

All That Is Alive

And all that came to be was alive with this life.

The Gospel

Almighty and everliving God,
you are the author of all things beautiful.

The Prayers of the People

When it's over, I want to say:
all my life I was a bride married to amazement.

Mary Oliver

*J*esus loves me, this I know, for the Bible tells me so."

I sang along with everyone else when I was growing up. But I was uncertain if it were true, and I was uncertain about many other things the Bible and the Sunday school teachers told me until my father told me it was truth. I am still uncertain about many things in precisely that way, though I cannot ask my father about it any longer.

"All that came to be was alive with his life." I believe this because my father believed it, and I believed him.

His favorite passage of the Holy Writ was the Prologue to the Gospel of John.

He decided somehow it would be a good idea for the youth choir—as some people referred to us—to recite dramatic readings of scripture. He made me and a dozen other young people in the church commit the Prologue to memory and perform it onstage in churches around the South. We saw ourselves as the vanguard of the Christian rock-and-roll movement and thought the notion we should stop in between our clearly powerful and penetrating versions of "modern youth music," the new music that was going to revolutionize the faith, was clearly ridiculous. And furthermore, we knew the idea was lame to the third power.

Except it turns out that the words, and then the Word itself, never left me. Everything I believe about everything I believe begins in those few paragraphs.

It was the sixties, and my father was discovering the front bits of the life of the music executive he was to become. He was discovering the inklings of his career as a writer and speaker across the country. He was also the head of the youth group at our local church, and he somehow managed to marry the three streams into a traveling youth group performing in churches, trying out new music and new forms while he spoke at the end of the set and found his not inconsequential voice.

My memories of him in those days are among the sweetest of him I have. With all the blessing and grace that came to either of us, and the both of us, both before he passed away and since—trusting that the dear ones who share my life now will understand this as I write it—the truth is, I would forsake everything in an instant to be able to return to those days, if I could again stand next him as he was then. I would even be willing to do dramatic readings if he still thought it was a good idea.

I love what my father became over the few years he had left. I worked alongside him in the business and traveled the country and the world with him, plowing through business meetings, sitting backstage, cheering him along, editing his lines sometimes, packing up and tearing down.

"In the beginning was the Word. The Word was with God and the Word was God. . . . And all that came to be was alive with this life."

All these years later, whenever I hear the words of that passage read, it comes to me again: Wherever there is life at all, then it is the Life and the Light of the whole world, the Life and the Light of the first Word ever spoken.

My father lived his whole life under the influence of those few words, I think. Even the parts of his life I cannot remember, the parts which come to me by way of story or letter or photograph in these thirty years since we could no longer reach him on the telephone or see him standing at the end of the driveway or hear his tiny voice on a stage or in our ear, the sum of those parts reminds me he truly believed all that was alive was alive with the Light of the world.

He would walk into a shop in Nantucket, and while the rest of us would see pretty stuff to take home, he would see that the eye of the buyer had somehow seen into the heart of the One Who Came Among Us.

He would read a book all of us already read. We would see its power, and he would see its pain. He would take us all to a party. We would have a grand time, and he would spend the afternoon in the backyard under a tree listening to someone whose heart was breaking and who had no one to listen to them.

He would spend his day at some large conference, being the gospel hero onstage in front of a few hundred or a few thousand people, and then call me long-distance at midnight to read a sentence from some obscure monk, a sentence calling him to humility.

All these years later, I have come to believe my father taught me this: If what you are looking at has any life at all, then that life is a reflection of the Light of the world. All that is alive is alive with *that* Life. Whenever you see light, it is *the* Light.

The Darkness will never overcome the Light. Evidently the Bible is right when it tells us so.

❧

I have lived a religious life.

Not to be confused with a pure and smooth and clean and unblemished life, but a religious life nonetheless. It has been a life lived within the frames and references and strictures and habits and practices of Christian religious folks in the times in which I have lived.

Some of the folks I have known sit on the evangelical end of this great long pew that we call the Church, others are more liturgical and sacramental. I have found most all of them over the years to be faithful and devout, loving and purposeful.

I am grateful for all of them, even the ones with whom I have had serious disagreements over the years. And they with me.

I question no one's piety at this point in my life.

❧

But I think I am ready to say this:

The point of all our religious life is to learn to live in the life of the

Spirit, according to the One Who Came. And the religious life can lead to a kind of transcendence. I know, I have been a witness when such a thing has taken place. But it can also lead only to itself if we who are religious are not careful.

I have seen what looks remarkably like the life of the Spirit lived by people without any signs of the trappings of the religious life as many of us know it and practice it and hold it dear. We who travel home to God on the road of the Christian religious must understand the destination is the life of the Spirit, the life of the Light. Religion, even the one we hold dear, is not a home, it is simply a road. Some of us believe it the only road, but it is only a road.

We will not be known as the children of the Holy One because we are successfully religious but because we learn to love in the Spirit and transmit the Light. We will not live a life in the Light because we know how to behave. We are meant to *live*—live *our* lives—in the Light of the kingdom that has already come. We are meant to live as though we are under the influence of the Light that is the life of the whole world.

I believe this. The Bible told me so. And so did my Dad.

Setting Up the Gym

But to all who would receive the good news . . .

The Gospel

*Be present, we pray,
with all those who seek to perfect the praises of your people.*

The Prayers of the People

*Whatever optimism I possess comes from knowing
that new people are brought into the world all the time,
and they come in singing.*

Jackson Browne

There is a church for sale in my neighborhood.
It is a beautiful old brick building in a quiet neighborhood of early-twentieth-century cottages and sidewalks lined by grand old trees. There is lovely stained glass, no doubt paid for over the years by people whose people grew up there, glass to honor those who walked this way before. The front steps have hollowed out places on their edges, a collective footprint of the walk of the faithful over many, many years.

Each time I drive by on worship days, I pass by slowly, following the directions of the security man they post in the middle of the street. I make the sign of the cross as I pass. I make it quickly so no one will see. They are Holiness folks of some sort, and I do not want them to take offense at what I make as an act of prayer in solidarity with them.

Their moving breaks my heart. Not because I have any vested interest but because the place itself is a holy place for a lot of people, even if I do not know them. Given the nature of our neighborhood, the building is likely to become a restaurant or a mall for artisans. At least I hope it will become at least some such thing. To tear the building down would be a tragedy.

I am an old church person.

I am moved by the great and grand worship spaces created for the glory of God. I hold them dear, and each time I visit one, I am drawn to the vision and the heart and the devotion of the people who built them and the people who make their way into them week after week, year after year, to offer their praise and worship to the One Who Made Us, the One Who is the center of all things. Such sacred spaces never fail to move me.

I have visited some of the great cathedrals of the world—London, Cologne, Paris, New York, San Francisco, New Orleans—and can still remember the sense of Presence I felt inside those walls, made sacred by the prayer and devotion of all those who walked this way before me. The road I have traveled has also led me into what must be hundreds of little chapels and sanctuaries all over this land.

Brick and mortar, wood and glass, big rooms and small ones, all of which gave me the same sense of Presence when I entered them or worshiped in them or spoke in them. I may not always see the Light of the world when I am there, but I know the Holy when the Holy is nearby. And it moves me.

When I was invited to travel to Kansas City to speak at Sunday morning services for a church that meets in a high school gym, I was a little unnerved.

Not only do I remember the great houses of worship in which I have walked, I remember being in high school and being a freshman point guard. Our coach may have uttered words of the Holy Presence while we were there, but I cannot come up with any of them. You can dress the thing up, but a gym smells like a gym.

In the first place, we were not going to meet in Kansas City but actually out in the suburbs west of the great town. And these days all suburbs look alike.

Have you ever noticed you can be in Buckhead or Burlingame or Reston or Brentwood or Naperville or Cary and not know whether you are outside Atlanta or San Francisco or Washington, DC, or Nashville or Chicago or Raleigh without consulting the boarding pass in your pocket?

All these suburbs look the same to me. There is no *there* there.

Sunday morning broke over the outskirts of Kansas City, and one of the nice people who invited me to speak picked me up at the hotel. We are going early, he told me, because he had to help set up. They had a quiet room for me—a green room, as the saying goes—if I wanted to be alone for the two hours required to turn a gym into a sanctuary. And he gave me a sticker with my name on it to wear so people would know who was the stranger in their midst.

Properly gentle-spirited, humble hired guru for the day I am supposed to be, I said, "Fine by me. I just want to be a blessing."

I did not go to the green room they had made for me. The notion that I was supposed to be somehow bothered by their activity made me nervous. I sat beside the door in the corner of the gym. From there I could watch the gym and the hallway while sipping tea and looking holy. (Sipping tea in a green room while looking holy does not matter at all if no one sees you.) People would stop from time to time to say hello, saying they were glad I had come to see them on this day of worship. I enjoyed that part.

They arrived in waves, scheduled and choreographed to give them time to do their particular tasks at the right time so that the room was made ready for worship. They hauled tables and brought in doughnuts, they rolled out the carpet and set up the chairs, they hung the lights and the curtains, they laid out study books on a table and spread out the crayons and the coloring books for the young ones, they made the coffee and set out the water bottles, they did sound checks and hung banners.

Pretty soon these people were going to act as though they were people of God, but first they were going to be roadies. As I watched them, I hummed that great hymn of the church—Jackson Browne's "The Load-Out"—a tune most of them were too young to have ever heard. "Let the roadies take the stage. . . ." I smiled the whole time—at them and the song. I moved my name badge to my right thigh as all the roadies in my life had taught me to do so that I would look cool.

Then the house band arrived.

Given the churches and the church folks I was around for much of my life, it was not always so, but these days my idea of a house band for Sunday morning is thirty professional voices robed in white, a pipe organ, the occasional baby grand piano, chanted psalms, and the hymns of Ralph Vaughn Williams and the Wesleys. A Bach cantata is suitable for feast days. A drum kit, three guitars, a synthesizer, a percussionist, three roving, microphone-toting backup singers, and song lyrics on the wall do not exactly say high and holy day to me. This is not theological, it is simply taste. I have heard rock-and-roll bands in church before—I was among the first people who ever brought one into a church.

I listened to the band warm up—the tuning, the sound checks. I watched the water bottles being placed in a row with names marked on them and the set lists being taped to the floor. My music business days came flooding back to me. And it made me smile.

Then the crowd came in to worship—to worship in this room made holy by their presence, by their having sought and then carried the Light they had seen in the days they had been apart into a space no more or less holy than any other concrete block building in any other faceless suburb.

When the service was finished, they offered me the green room again. I chose to return to my chair by the door to watch them tear down. You get more hugs and greetings if you do so. "Pack it up and tear it down," Mr. Browne and I sang along together in my head, while people said nice things to me.

According to the literature they had spread out on the tables, they were off to feed the hungry, hold little meetings in their houses all week, say the prayers that sanctify the day, take care of children after school, collect clothes for the homeless, and visit the sick and imprisoned. I might have signed up, but it was time for me to go home.

According to their lights, the Light of the world was not confined to the building in which they gathered up each week to say thank you to the One Who Made Us and sent us the Light.

There is something to be said for the great and beautiful and holy and sacred spaces built by the faithful. There is also something to be said for places that are made holy and sacred by the devotion of the ones who turn them into such each week.

The thing that is to be said about them both is this: Thanks be to God. And God bless us every one.

✺

I myself have a deep affection for the great buildings we have made to honor and glorify the One Who Made Us. And if the choice for me on a Sunday is a cathedral or a gym, I am pretty set in my ways at this point.

But here is the truth: The Light of the world does not live in a building where we worship, whether the room is a great cathedral or a suburban gym, no matter what we say we hold dear, no matter where we attend the next Sabbath day.

We do not gather up on Sundays, wherever we gather up, to *find* the Light. We come to *celebrate* the Light. The Light is already everywhere we have been all week. We are simply pausing with others who want to acknowledge we have seen the Light yet again in the last few days. The Light of the world is already in the world. We simply gather up on Sundays to say we have seen it within us and without us and all around us, and that we are grateful, and that we are at one with the others who are looking for the places where holes have been punched in the darkness all around us.

The places we worship are not the only places where the Light can be seen, they are simply the places where we go to rejoice in the glow of it.

The risk for all of us who call ourselves by the Holy Name is that we think we are housing the Light and then carrying the Light into the world. More likely, the Light travels the other way. We are not called to protect the Light in a building we call a church. We are called to be the Light of the world. I would not choose a gym in the suburbs. But I will not deny its holiness on any given Sabbath.

I will still be heartbroken when they sell the church in my neighborhood.

Holy spaces, spaces made holy by the prayer and worship of those who walked and prayed and sang there, will always matter to me. I hope to never fail to give thanks for them and be inspired by them and to imitate them.

But when other people are thinking about the appetizers in the restaurant to inevitably be housed there, I will be thinking about the ones whose names I do not know, the ones who once gathered up there to celebrate the Light of the world among us.

I will be grateful for the fact of the building itself. I will be even more grateful for its celebrants, wherever they are on that day. They will be out there somewhere, going through the world singing. Looking for the Light, just like me.

First, Go and
Make Peace

Before you leave your gift at the altar,
go and make peace with your brother.

The Gospel

Break down the walls that separate us, we pray.

The Prayers of the People

The shortest distance between two points is a straight line—
A straight line like "I love you."

Ralph Keyes

I *n the beginning, someone got their feelings hurt.*

Two of our friends in the neighborhood took offense at some slight, or series of slights. It caused no small amount of tension within our little band, a band of eight couples who had been friends for years, sharing movies and birthdays, suppers and holidays, weddings and births and deaths, parties and picnics, swim days and crawfish boils. For weeks and then into months, there were cutting remarks and angry looks, unspoken words of frustration and unacknowledged acts of unkindness. There were tears and mutterings, text messages and e-mails filled with resignation and anger and hurt and self-righteousness.

All the while, our little band of friends gathered up on occasion as was our way, all of us trying to rise above the dark of it all. Then three of our group decided to walk toward the light a bit in order to push back against the dark.

Around the same time, my mother passed away.

(Thank you for that little murmur, especially those of you who knew Miss Peggy and are only just now hearing the news. She was very ill for a very long time, and her time had come. She is probably leading the heavenly host in show tunes even as I write and you read. Smile, my friends, she lived a lovely life.)

My sister wrote and delivered a lovely eulogy. My decision not to try and share the stage with my sister and my brother who officiated at the service was one of the two or three best decisions I ever made. They were lovely and smart and tender and gracious. Any poor attempt on my part to add to what they had to say would have been a waste of time and energy, and most certainly would have taken away from their artful, thoughtful hard work for the day.

My brother's attention to those in the room who had loved Miss Peggy for all her life was sweet and gentle and rich. My sister's eulogy was powerful enough that people who never even met Miss Peggy laughed until they cried and then cried until they started laughing again.

My sister told a not-often-told story about our mother.

Some years ago, one of Miss Peggy's dearest friends for some forty years, a friend who had lunch with my mother and a small group every week, got offended by some bit of something and began to withdraw from the group. Whatever it was, it seems to have gone unsaid. Or perhaps it was only said around the edges and never directly or perhaps never really listened to. As years went by, none of them, as near as we know, ever had much more than a guess as to what small bit of something caused the rift.

What we do know now are the words in the copy of a letter my sister found, a letter my mother once wrote to her friend.

"I am writing you again," she said, "hoping this is the year when you will forgive us and come back to us. We need never talk about what happened if you do not want to, but know that if you call me, I will get in my car and come to you right away, and all will be well.

"Perhaps this is the year," she wrote.

The year never came. And now they are both gone.

After some months of gnashing of teeth and wringing of hands and wondering about what to do, three courageous ones in our neighborhood decided the time had come to try and reconcile. It was not an easy thing for them to choose to do. All of them were just as hurt by the whole business as were the rest of us.

When you are right, it is hard to say you might not be. And we are always right, are we not? We all see everything in the clearest light, always know the right thing to do, never say the wrong thing, always do what is right and proper, yes?

We are somehow predisposed to think that the fact the other person cannot see how right we are is their problem, which is a fine posture until you start to lose friends. Suddenly, being the rightest person on the planet does not matter anywhere near as much as having your friends back. But admitting that single thing is often the hardest thing of all to admit. The shortest of distances can sometimes be the hardest to travel.

The three friends decided to sit one evening in one of our back gardens and talk. They made great pains, I was told, to lay their hurt out on the table and then to listen to the hurt coming from the other side of the table. Of all the blamed things, they listened to each other and tried to make peace with each other.

What they heard come back to them were tales of hurt and woe, some real and some imagined, some more than a little difficult to say or hear or understand. But they listened nonetheless. There were tears and confessions and straight lines and laughter. There were signs of courage and heart and disappointment and love. No doubt there was clumsiness and awkwardness and more than a few unintended consequences.

But perhaps there was Light.

Truth be told, it did not work out in the end. A few months later, our group shrank and all of our hearts were a little bit broken. Still are, methinks, at least mine is. I am sure that I am not alone. But the story still makes me hopeful.

I have come to believe this: When it comes to making peace, the result matters less than the attempt. We are not called to solve everything before we come to the altar, we are called to go and offer peace to our brother or our sister before we offer our gift at the altar.

"Enter any house that will welcome you," said the One Who Came. "Share their meal, tend their sick"—the sick of heart as well as the sick of body, one must assume—"and there is where you will find the Kingdom."

A back garden, a table under a tree, a plate of cheese, and a pitcher of water will do. And *listening to* is the same as *tending to*, methinks.

Am I the only one in the world who wakes up far too many mornings angry at some crowd of folks or some particular folks? Am I the only one who is so intent on shouting at the darkness I cannot see the Light?

I wake up some days so angry with the folks in the other political party I can barely breathe. (My party is the yellow dog one, he admitted, as though no one had yet noticed.) I also wake up some days still holding on tightly to some long ago slight, probably unintentional, likely imagined, but holding tightly enough my hands hurt. No telling how such things affect my heart.

I also stand in sanctuaries and talk about our brothers and sisters of other faiths and never talk to them at all, not seriously ever making any steps toward reconciliation. I carry on great long theological arguments with those who do not see the Light in the same way I do, thereby accomplishing little more than prolonging the darkness between us. I rail against the injustice others do and never open my eyes to the places where I am unjust or unfair or unaware or unfeeling.

Am I the only one?

To be sure, three friends sitting down in a back garden on a spring night will not change the world. Everything between was not resolved that night, and it is clear that the situation may never be resolved in the way we all hoped.

One little spark of reconciliation in a small neighborhood in a small Southern city is not likely to chase away all the dark of the world, even all the dark in our little group of friends. But I know the garden they sat in, the one in our neighborhood with the lights hung in the maple tree, the lights that come on at dusk each evening. And for that evening, as they sat in the light from the tree, they sat in the light of reconciliation. They sat in the Light of the very daughters and sons of the One Who Made Us. They did their best to offer peace to each other.

I know most all of us tend very small gardens anyway. Even so, I am called to do my best to see the Light and be the Light in the garden to which I have been given—for the sake of the One Who Came, for the sake of those who come and go from day to day and night to night, for the sake of my own sweet self.

"Before you offer your gift at the altar, first go and make peace with your brother or sister." Simple words, often a difficult task. But a necessary one. The One Who made us does not require results, rather it is effort to which we are called. Success is not the object of the exercise. Sacrifice is the object of the exercise. Even if all we sacrifice is our own sweet selves.

These days I think often about those with whom I need to make peace before I offer my gift, the ones for whom I am to punch a hole in the mutual darkness we have somehow managed to create. And I think of my friends, and I think about my mother and her friends.

Ah, Miss Peggy, "Perhaps this is the year."

Bearing Fruit

I am appointing you to bear fruit that will last.

The Gospel

Forgive us when we come here for solace and not for strength.

The Prayers of the People

There were times when I felt
that something better and truer than my words
was speaking through my words.

Frederick Buechner

*T*he spiritual life requires holding two opposite notions at the same time.

We are often given two truths and are meant to try and figure out a single posture which allows us to hold them both.

According to the Revised Common Lectionary, a pattern for reading the Holy Writ we Anglican folk follow whenever we worship, the Story of Us All unfolds in the same pattern year after year.

The Lectionary also guides the Lutherans and the Methodists and the Catholics. It also directs the Disciples of Christ (a name which begs the question of whether or not people who take the Eucharist each Sunday might be disciples of someone else.) The pattern is followed by at least one of the four varieties of Presbyterians, though I can never remember which one. Cooperative Baptists as well. I generally am willing to settle for a reasonable Baptist since cooperative remains a distant dream here on the buckle of the Bible Belt where I live. Perhaps some of them are wondering if they will ever find a Bible-believing Episcopalian.

One of the first notches on the Belt was cut by my great-grandfather who helped start the Nazarene denomination on the site of the church with the big steeple you see behind the stadium in the panoramic television shots of Nashville. Because the Nazarenes do not use the Lectionary I do not know what they talk about through the Easter season, but we Lectionary folks are being told once again we are to go and bear fruit. Jesus goes on about it for weeks.

This past Easter, after the longest time—somewhere between the fifty days of Easter we are living now and my more than fifty years of being a churchman—I heard something I think is close to what the One Who Came Among Us was trying to tell us on His last night at table with His friends, and tell to us by extension, on one fine morning here on the buckle of the Bible Belt.

"Go and bear fruit," He keeps saying.

He speaks these words in the midst of conversations about love one another and love each other the way I have loved you, and love each other the way the Father loves me. "Go and love one another, go and bear fruit."

What is the fruit He is expecting, for Pete's sake, and what does it look like if I bear some of it?

In a conversation I was in not too long ago, these words of the Christ were read. As we began to talk together about bearing fruit, there was a lot of conversation about vocation and how we spend our lives and what we do with our work and our time.

There was the inevitable talk about pruning and the hope we could see pruning as a gift. Words like ministry and calling and service came up a fair amount. There was very earnest talk—spoken and unspoken, I remember and suspect—about all the things we think we are to do in the name of bearing fruit.

There was quite a bit of talk about branches that do not bear fruit, branches lopped off and cast into the fire and how afraid some of us are—including me, maybe even especially me—of not being worthy of being considered to be a branch on the vine and ending up going up in flames.

My mind began to run through all the things we are taught we might do for the love of the One Who Made Us, and all those gifts given by the Spirit and some of them given even to me—all the work to be done in the name of the Holy—and I started to worry, of course. I remembered all the times and places I failed to be the teacher and the minister and the prophet and the worker I ought to be. I started to get uneasy and ashamed, and I began to think I could hear the sound of clippers clipping and pruners pruning. And was that smoke I could smell in the distance?

I suspect I am not the only one who hears those echoes in their head when we talk about Jesus' call to us to bear fruit. I held the conversation in my head for a week, in one hand so to speak, trying to work my way through to the other end. Then I did something that some would consider unusual for an Episcopalian. I did a little Bible study work.

And ended up holding a new thing in my other hand.

Saint Paul had popped into my head. Honestly, Saint Paul.

I find myself as mystified by some of what Paul had to say as anyone you have ever known. With the exception of a few verses in Ephesians and Philippians where I think he must have lost his way and wandered into the Gospel for a few minutes, I tend to argue with him all the time. Most of us simply wander into the Gospel from time to time, I think.

I rolled my way through all of the lists of the spiritual gifts annotated by Paul in Romans and Corinthians and wherever else they are found—wisdom, knowledge, faith, healing, miracles, exhortation, discernment, tongues, ministry, teaching, some to be apostles, some gifts for evangelists or prophets, pastors, teachers, for exhortation and administration and on and on, all those things which pop into our heads when we think about bearing fruit. We who sit in the pews have long been taught these are the things that measure the fruit we are to be. We have been taught this by nearly every preacher who ever preached a sermon or gave a homily. Our culture has reinforced it. What we *do* is everything, what we *be* is less highly regarded.

Whenever we face questions about bearing fruit, about being recognized as one of the friends of the Holy, we think about what we have done and are doing, about we have not done and what we cannot do. We spend our lives in fear of the pruning equipment and the fire pit.

Then I noticed the apostle Paul was the only New Testament writer who ever attempted to say what the fruits of the life of the Spirit are. His words drew my attention because for the first time it occurred to me I had spent much of my life measuring my bearing of fruit or lack thereof by looking at the wrong blame list.

"These are the fruits of the Spirit," he writes to the Galatians—why he did not share this with the Romans and the rest we will likely never know. Maybe the letters got lost in the mail. "These are the fruits of the spirit: joy and peace and forbearance and kindness and goodness and faithfulness and gentleness and self-control and love."

Deep, deep breath.

No ministry, no witness, no success, no changing of the world. No churches to build, no classes to teach, no missionary trips to make. No board memberships, no miracles, no recognition as a prophet.

This is how they will know you are a friend of the Holy—by your joy, peace and forbearance, kindness and goodness, faithfulness and gentleness and self-control. By the way you *be*, not by the what you *do*. By the way you love, one might say, not by the way you work. These are the fruits of the life of the One Who Came.

Well, my goodness, I thought, *I can do some of that.* Maybe a lot of that. Maybe I am not destined for the embers after all.

I am not much of a prophet, but I might yet learn to become faithful in my attendance to prayer and worship and the needs of those who are given to me. I am not a miracle worker, but I can share my joy at sharing the Easter with the folks at the American Cathedral in Paris, a joyous memory at which I weep even all these weeks later.

I cannot speak in tongues a lick—my Southern accent not withstanding—but I might aspire to becoming as patient as the day is long. I surely do not have the courage and dedication displayed by those who follow the call to be pastors, but I might learn to show more kindness and generosity and presence to those who are closest to me.

I cannot be a missionary by a long shot—too many bugs and too much shyness and too much strange food and no *New York Times*—but there is a possibility I may muster up the strength to walk through my world with modesty and humility and hope.

The gift of administration? I could not balance my checkbook if I could find it. Not to mention that the only time in my years of being a churchman I was elected to the board I was asked not to come back after three meetings. I am not very good at building consensus, but is there a possibility I may be able to learn to make peace?

Do you hear what I am hearing? Or have I merely come along with my bushel and covered everything up once again?

To bear fruit is to *be* as the Holy has been to us—loving and joyful, peaceful and patient, kind and good and gentle, faithful and modest and generous. Others will know we love the One Who Made Us and the One Who Came Among Us by the way we treat with one another, not by the way we work on each other.

To bear fruit is to hold a posture rather than to accomplish a task. It is a set of things to *be* rather than a set of things to *do*.

I think the vision I should keep in mind when I pay attention to the call to bear fruit is not necessarily to live as the teacher or the miracle worker or the healer or the prophet. It is to become one who welcomes, sheds tears, forgives, washes feet, to live as one who is gentle and kind and tolerant. That is how we know He loved us, how we know God loves us. And that is how anyone else will know I love God and the One

Who was sent, how they will know that I am a disciple, a follower of the Christ. I cannot ever *do* enough for them to know this truth about me. The road of proving myself leads to hedge clippers and charcoal. I can only live in a way that the light of the Light reflects from me. And then, maybe they will know.

Maybe only then, will I have borne fruit.

I am not in charge of making sweet plums that shine in the sun, I am asked only to be one.

I am to be sweet and gentle and ripe and full of the light and the warmth of the sun and the magic that makes life possible. I am to be good enough that you grin when you see me headed in your direction. And if I am, then people will know that I am loved and that I love them in return. Only then will something better and truer than words have a chance to shine through.

I cannot hear such good news without a powerful desire to lie down and giggle, even when we live in the valley of the shadow of death.

It Is Our Turn

Do not think too much of yourself
when you have only done your duty.

The Gospel

You are worthy at all times to be praised by happy voices.

The Prayers of the People

I have never, ever thought
that Latin chant opposes personal prayer.
It is simply personal prayer as part of a total community.

John Dominic Crossan

One of my road rules is simple: hotels, not homes.

Most of the time when I travel to speak at a retreat or a workshop, I stay in a hotel room or a lodge or retreat center where the event is being held. From time to time, my hosts will suggest I stay in someone's home. The suggestion is always one part hospitality and one part cost-saving. I completely understand both.

However, my answer is always no, always said gently, even though very emphatic. I am far too shy, far too introverted, far too exhausted at the end of a day talking to strangers to go somewhere and be the entertaining visiting speaker when the day is done.

Unless the road takes me to Raleigh, North Carolina.

My friends Lib and Tom live in Raleigh.

I have known them a long time and worked on projects with them over the years, ranging from conferences to retreats to workshops to publishing. Tom has become such a good friend to me I have been known to mutter under my breath from time to time, "I need me some Tom Campbell," and pick up the telephone.

The first time I stayed with them was by chance. I was to work in rural Virginia and needed to fly to Raleigh and drive to Virginia the next day, work for three days, and come back to Raleigh to catch a plane for home. I was telling Tom about the trip on the telephone, and he said I should fly in, stay at his house, and go on from there.

Lib and Tom have a big house, and I could stay upstairs and never even see them if I wanted to avoid company. And then Tom threw in the use of his convertible at no charge and I was in. He was offering hospitality, and I was needing to cut costs. (I know, I know.)

I said yes and flew to Raleigh. He sent someone to pick me up and I went to their house. As it turned out, I was not even the only traveler staying at their house that night. But because they were not the hosts for the event I was working on the weekend, I was under no pressure to act as though I was anyone other than myself, and the evening passed peacefully. They even invited mutual friends for dinner and asked me to read from the new pile of sentences I was working on. Their dog slept in the room with me. He knew better than to trust writers under his roof.

The next morning I went down for coffee, and the household was up, the other guest included, and they were all standing around the big island in the kitchen, reading the papers and eating food at a ridiculously unholy hour and talking about the news of the day before and the work of the day to come. When the time came to go our separate ways, Tom said, "Well, we should make our office before we go."

They broke out the prayer books and spread them round the counter. Together we said the morning office and the psalms appointed for the day and said the collects in unison and lifted up concerns, thanksgivings, petitions, and intercessions while naming names aloud. We said the prayer that Jesus taught us to pray. We waded into the great river of prayer that has gone on for centuries before us, dried our feet off, and went out the door to love and serve the Lord and to "live our lives so that those for whom love is a stranger might find in us generous friends."

I spent some time in the Methodist part of the Church and learned something about the founding light, John Wesley, that I did not know.

If you spent the night at Wesley's house you had to attend morning prayer and evening prayer, however you spent your day. No attendance to the prayers, no food for you at mealtime. You could sleep there when it was time to sleep, you could eat there when it was time to eat, but only if you prayed when it was time to pray.

Lib and Tom were not quite as strict, but I would not blame them if they had been.

Two particular bits of liturgical practice have kept the Church alive for the last two thousand years.

One is the Eucharist—the *weekly* gathering up of the faithful to share in the body and blood of Christ.

The second is the praying of the *daily* office by both clergy and laity. The blessed ordinariness makes it matter the most, maybe more than anything else any of us can do, especially any of us liturgical Christians—Catholics, Anglicans, Episcopalians, Lutherans, and others who are called to this particular duty.

These ways of worship and prayer have sustained the Church for centuries. They are the only two common threads. These practices will only cease to matter if folks like you and me no longer pay attention to the duty to which we were called and to which we said "I will" at our baptisms.

But we do not hear that very much, not in the world of *Christian* conversation we hear on the radio, see on our televisions, receive from our pulpits, or read in our newspapers and magazines and the blog sites we follow.

If it is mentioned at all, we more often hear that this ancient way of prayer does not matter at all.

I believe prayer builds upon itself.

"Follow the pattern of the sound words you have been given," Paul wrote to his friends, "guard the truths that have been given us by the Spirit who dwells within us." This was written by a man who said such prayer all his life, as did all of the followers of Yahweh who proceeded him.

There are many folks who say the old ways of prayer are dead. They declare it rote prayer with no meaning, prayer which cannot be heard and remains dry and lifeless and not of the Spirit. These are the things generally said by those who are certain they know exactly the things one should say to God, and the ways one should say them, in order to get the Creator of the Universe to answer correctly to one's beck and call. Those folks are generally certain they need not bend to discipline of any sort. They also claim to completely understand the ways of the Unknowable One whose name they claim.

According to the Gospel, the apostles once said to the One Who Came, "Increase our faith." After confusing them, and all the rest of us, with a parable about a mustard seed—He then offered this to them, "Do what is given you. When you get to thinking you have done more than your share, remind yourselves you are only doing your duty."

You and I are the inheritors of the call to liturgical duty going back to the beginning of the Church itself. History suggests we are sustaining the very life of the Church.

"Be still before the Lord and wait patiently," the psalmist whispers, "wait upon the Lord and keep His ways."

"Write down the vision," writes the prophet, "make it plain and simple, the vision will not lie. If it moves slowly, wait for it and it will come true."

In recent weeks I was a guest lecturer for college students at a Church of Christ university, a bastion of evangelical presence and thought, where they are now saying *Lauds* as part of the weekly chapel program. I also led a three day retreat about the ancient ways of prayer and the Rule of St. Benedict with a small crowd of millionaire businessmen. I got to spend a weekend with an emerging church crowd who asked me to lead them in the prayers at *Vespers* of all things, a contemplative service they think they have invented. I had a three-hour conversation with a Southern Baptist minister, a man whose flock is currently 8,726 strong and whose campus is larger than where I went to high school and college combined. He wanted to talk about liturgical practice, though he was whispering when he spoke to me.

According to the prophet, "I am doing a work in your days you would not believe if told," are the words of the One Who Made Us.

These prayers matter, even when others say they do not, and even when you and I and others who say them wonder if we are even still a part of the conversation in the American, Western, twenty-first century, megachurch, emerging church, marketing program church at all anymore.

℘

There is a setting on my alarm for only Thursday of each week—5:20: to the Allens.

For some years, a group of folks in my neighborhood has gathered to say the morning office, part of the ancient liturgical offering of daily prayer and praise and worship offered to the One Who Made Us. We say it on our own most days, but once each week for some fifteen years now, we gather on Thursdays to say the prayers together, for the love of God, for the love of our own sweet selves, and for the love of our neighbors who are still asleep in their beds, no matter how far away they may be.

We are not alone.

Every morning, whether we realize it or not, a great cloud of witnesses does not begin their day's work until they have offered the ancient prayers. Some of them are monks and nuns and priests, but a fair number of them are folks like you and me. Folks who have come to believe the darkness of the night they have passed through is not truly broken until they have raised their voices and lifted their hands and rang their bells and lit their candles up as the dawn breaks. They punch a hole that only prayer and worship can punch into the darkness that appears to surround us.

Anyone who participates in these holy acts of devotion is never alone. The sun rises in the east each day and moves its way across the fields and cities and towns, and every few minutes someone, or a group of someones, attends to their altar and punches a little hole in the darkness each day, making room for and honoring the Light coming in among us.

Perhaps, as Thomas Merton writes of his first few days with the monks of Gethsemani, "This is the center of America. I had wondered what was holding this country together, what has been keeping the universe from cracking in pieces and falling apart."

Perhaps the center of the whole praying universe is a block and a half from my house and meets on Thursdays. Perhaps it is in Raleigh, North Carolina.

Perhaps it is on the street where you live. Or it could be.

Billy

When did we see you?

The Gospel

Accept our repentance
for our blindness to human need and suffering.

The Prayers of the People

The world is full of people who have stopped
listening to themselves or have listened only to their neighbors
to learn what they ought to do, how they ought to behave,
and what the values are that they should be living for.

Joseph Campbell

There was a knock at our door one morning.

The lovely and fine woman to whom I am married went to the door, pulled the curtain back and found what could only be called a character standing on the porch. He had graying hair in dreadlocks, a striking, sharply featured face, a charming grin. He was dressed in a baseball cap on backwards, T-shirt with the sleeves cut off, dungarees that were too long and rolled at the ankles, and work boots.

"I noticed you have some weeding somebody ought to do," he said. "I thought you might want me to take care of it for you." She said it would be all right she supposed. She locked the door behind her, and he went to work.

A couple of hours later, he knocked at the door again and wanted to know if she could make him a sandwich for breakfast. And coffee with a lot of sugar would be nice, too. She said yes, of course. When you grow up in the South that we did, you know that such work comes with lunch, no negotiating required.

He worked three or four hours all together, doing good work, and then he knocked at the door again. I was home from my scribbling for the day by then and had seen him working and the situation had been explained to me. "Can I get you to drop me off?" he asked.

His destination being only about four minutes away, it seemed easy enough. I told him I would give him a lift, and off we went to the ATM to get his wages and to drop him safe home.

His name was Billy.

About the same time, a letter arrived at our house from the church we attend.

They encouraged us to give more money this year to help them give more money and aid to the poor. We have known these church folks for twenty years. A very active and energetic and thoughtful group, they have done a fair amount of very good work for people in our city who live in unfortunate circumstances. They are forever organizing food drives for stocking the shelves at the food bank, gathering up clothing for hand out at the local shelter, looking for housing arrangements for homeless folks, and spearheading political action in the city. The parish has done good work for people in other parts of the world. An orphanage in South America owes its existence in large measure to contributions and work projects from members of our parish.

But they never found Billy.

When we first met Billy, he was sleeping outside a few days a week under the picnic table on the porch of the youth building of the church across the street, sometimes on the floor in a basement where he swept out the premises during the day, sometimes under the stairwell of a local entertainment venue where he picked up trash in the parking lot in return for breakfast. His contact with them largely consisted of trying to be awake and gone before they discovered him each day and threw him off the porch.

He has a cousin in the neighborhood where he is allowed to sleep inside when cold weather comes, but they charge him twelve dollars a night. He is illiterate, though he has a high school diploma and went to college on a track scholarship at a local university. He has a shed where he keeps tools, and he has a niece who lives nearby where he can stay from time to time.

Billy's life has changed some now.

He works for us in our garden one or two days a week. Truth be told, we were tired of doing all the yard work and are happy to have the help. A few dollars and some coffee and breakfast and a ride seem a good trade to us. This spring the garden was in better shape than in several springs, the roses were brighter, the monkey grass was thicker, and the palm grasses were neat and tidy and coming up strong and clear when the warm weather came.

He has knocked on enough doors in our neighborhood and used us enough as reference now to have relatively steady work at a dozen or more houses around us. He has achieved a kind of fame on our neighborhood mailing list, enough for a number of us to keep up with him and tell him who is looking for him to come and mulch or lay brick or haul stuff. He keeps his tools, many of them our tools, in the *alleé* alongside our house and comes and goes whenever he needs them. Our power washer spent the last six months moving from house to house. Whether or not the machine was homesick was a running joke between

Billy

us for months. If our gate is locked, he goes round to the other side and comes over the fence and through the hedge. We keep a card with a picture of him and our telephone numbers stuck to the back porch in case the police come by and suspect he is up to some criminal activity. They surprise and surround him in one of our back gardens every few months, simply because the color of his skin makes him look like he does not belong there.

Billy has a new fan someone bought for him, though none of us knows where he keeps it from night to night. A local clinic makes sure he gets medicines for his kidney condition, and one of our neighbors keeps the schedule and makes sure he gets there on time for his check-ups. He has a cell phone one of his customers keeps paid up for him so we can find him, and he walks her dog in return. One of us recently spent a couple of days helping him get a birth certificate and settle some court issues so that he can have a photo ID for the first time in twenty years, something he has to have in order to receive the help our government can offer him.

He still sometimes shows up late and on the wrong day and still plays the numbers and still needs a meal or two most days. He still knocks on our door every once in a while and wants us to spot him twelve dollars. (Why he always asks for twelve dollars is a mystery, but it is

85

always what he asks for.) He keeps a stash of stuff he has rescued from trash piles, stuff he plans to take to local yard sales, and he keeps a pile of clothes and other stuff on our front porch and two or three others in the neighborhood. He has an annoying habit of showing up in the back garden whenever you have company, but then family is family, is it not?

But thanks to his neighbors, our neighbors, his life is changed and changed for the better.

When I think about us church folks, I wonder at our collective and general way of being with the poor.

I wonder about the way we do not open the door to the Billys of the world while we head to committee meetings to plan our mission trips to a small village in Latin America. I wonder about our clothing drives where we drop off clothes at the church and never meet the people who come to pick them up. I wonder about the way we drop off food in bags in the narthex and never look into the eyes of those who are hungry. I wonder about the way we drive past the poor on the way to give our money to people whose job or ministry is to take care of the poor on our behalf.

I do not wonder that we are not doing good. I wonder about the fact that we do not see our neighbor at all.

In our city, as in a number of others around the world, homeless people sell newspapers on the corner.

It is a way for people who are struggling to make a little money and take care of themselves. It is a way for them to regain some pride and some dignity.

But one of the most important bits of the whole enterprise to me is the way it brings the poor out of the shadows. We see them when we stop at a stoplight. We have vendors we buy from every week, and we know their names. We honk when we pass, and they wave or flash the peace sign. They are no longer invisible.

They are dangerously close to becoming our neighbor.

"When did we see you," asked Peter. "When did we see you naked or alone or hungry or thirsty or imprisoned?"

When *did* we see the One Who Came Among Us? When did we even look? Or look closely enough to look Him in the eye?

I worry about us church folks.

I worry when we do not open the door. I worry when we drive past people who need our help on the way to places where we talk about people who need our help. I worry when we do not see the Christ among us.

And I worry about Billy.

Billy is a mess, always has been, always will be.

Some of the mess is his own fault. He drinks too much and plays the numbers too much and cannot keep his stories straight too much. But some of the fault cannot be laid at his feet. For him to be passed from grade to grade to a track scholarship, for churches to chase him from under their picnic tables, for the police to stop him whenever they see him, for him to not qualify for government aid because he cannot read the forms—these things are not his fault.

But we drive past the Billys, and when we do not notice them we make the mess even worse, in spite of the money we give to the churches asking us to give more. I do not doubt the church folks will do good things with the money, many important things we could not do by ourselves. But I do worry we are missing the Billys simply because we do not open our eyes to them.

∽

We once had to move my mother from one apartment to another in the assisted living facility she came to call her last home. I hired Billy for the day to come and help us move furniture and haul boxes. He told me later he thought about sleeping in our backyard on the night before to make sure he was there on time for the day's work. He does not have an alarm clock or access to a wake-up call, and it is a thirty minute walk to my place.

My brother came to help, and there was a moment when we three were walking back down the hall and the two of them were some twenty feet ahead of me. They were laughing and joking, punching each other's arms as though they had known each other for years. It made me grin to watch them as I followed along. I suspect my brother never met a Billy before. They laughed together the whole day through. From time to time my brother will ask me how Billy is doing.

At the end of the three days of moving, I drove Billy home, and I thanked him for his hard work and his kindness to my mother.

"This is what you do, Robert. We're all family," Billy said.

I guess we are.

"When did we see you?" And why do we keep turning our heads?

We who claim the Name should open our eyes and not just our wallets. It is right to open our pantries and our closets, but we should open the door. Billy might be standing there, and he needs us.

And, the Dear One would tell us, we need to see the Christ standing there, or at least see Billy.

Driving Past Community

Why do you eat with the publicans and the sinners?

The Gospel

Forgive us
for all our false judgements
and our prejudice and contempt
toward those who differ from us.

The Prayers of the People

We live in a desert with many lonely travelers
who are looking for a moment of peace,
for a fresh drink and for a sign of encouragement
so that they can continue
their mysterious search for freedom.

Henri Nouwen

I *am going to tell you a story I have never told anyone before.*

A writer can write a story he believes points to the truth and may not yet see the truth of the story when he has finished, until he has listened for a while and let the story grow into itself. I may have not gotten this one right, but I am drawn to tell it anyway.

It is about my beloved father.

My father was named Bob Benson. For those of you who know anything about the Christian music business—yes, he was *that* Bob Benson. He was a minister, a writer, a Christian publisher, an influential person in the Nazarene community, a well-traveled preacher, a self-described contemplative before many folks in his circles ever even heard the word, and a gentle, poetic soul. He died far too young, at the age of fifty-six. He died with much of his music still in him through no fault of his own. He certainly did not hold back anything, he simply ran out of time.

My mom and dad had a group of friends made up of the men and women they grew up with at First Church of the Nazarene at 510 Woodland Street in Nashville. Lord in heaven, did they love each other—those eight or ten families—and encourage each other and hold each other up and bear each other's burdens. Most of them came from the same neighborhoods, attended the same schools, celebrated each other's weddings, and raised their families together. These folks pretty much believed and lived out of a common set of theological beliefs their whole lives. They were the first ones to tell me the Story and teach me its ways, for which I remain more grateful than I can say.

My family also had another set of friends. Both my mom and my dad were dear and deep friends with a lot of Christian music business folks, folks whose names you might know. I could give you a list, but I am afraid you would think I was just name-dropping.

We lived in a big house along the Cumberland River in Hendersonville, twenty miles north of Nashville, a couple of miles by water from Johnny Cash's place. Let the record show, the Bensons were there before the Cashes were. I even remember when Johnny was building their house. It was back in the days when Hendersonville was still a small town. It is now as close to being Buckhead or Cary or some other suburb as it can possibly be. I can hardly bear to go there.

Some portion of our family's two sets of friends came to our house almost every week. They came to eat and talk and laugh and swim and play tennis. Or to sleep over when they were in town to make a record or shoot pictures for album covers. They came to celebrate their children's weddings or share the holidays.

It was a joyful thing, a pure gift to grow up in such a place.

We lived five miles down a gravel road, and in those days there were only a dozen or so houses between us and the main road through town.

As the years went by, I found out that along the road during the time we lived there, there were three divorces, a man who died of a heart attack leaving a wife and two children behind, two cases of child abuse, and a bankruptcy. There were people whose children struggled with alcohol and drugs, people whose careers stalled, people whose weekly practice did not include going to houses of worship for one reason or another. And who knows what stories there were to be told among the parents of the schoolmates we had?

Yet with one or two exceptions, none of those people ever came to our house for a party or for grilling out or to have a swim from our dock or go water skiing with us on the weekends. We waved at our neighbors as we drove by—the publicans and the sinners—on our way to town to see our Christian friends or to pick them up at the airport and bring them home to make Christian music.

"What is this?" says the captain to Jonah while the storm is raging all round. "You are asleep? Do you not see the storm? At least make a plea to your god, for crying out loud."

(If you are checking your New International Version to see if I quoted scripture correctly, remember I warned you that paraphrasing is one of my habits. As it is for some other folks, I reckon.)

My great friend and fine writer Reuben Welch once said he is quite certain people need Jesus. "But most of the time," he said, "They just need someone to be Jesus to them."

In the category of being Jesus to anyone, my father was not the Messiah, though we used to tease him he might be. Behind his back, we called him Saint Bob. My mother was not Mother Mary either, and as much as we siblings love each other, none of us would put any of us forward as some great spiritual master. But one of us indeed might have been a fairly good stand-in for the Christ while sitting in a circle with some of those folks who lived up and down our road, those folks we hardly knew.

"Wherever two or three are gathered, I will be with you," the Story tells us the One Who Came Among Us to sit with publicans and sinners said. And where did we ever go—you and I—when we did not do so in His name, in the name of the One Who Came Among Us? Therefore, where do we ever go when we are not to look for the Christ in the room or maybe even be the Christ in the room? Or down the road?

It indeed makes me nervous to talk about my family in this way. I have never known kinder, more gentle, more deeply loving people in my life. I remain very aware, almost daily, of how lovely and tender was the place I grew up. And my great hope in the telling of this story is that those who loved our family most will not misunderstand me. But I do think that some of what we were taught by the Church caused us to misunderstand another something else the Church is trying to teach us: we will be not known as followers of the Christ because we avoid the publicans and sinners. We will be known as followers of the Christ because we invite them over to ski and stay over for hamburgers.

The number of people to whom my entire family was kind and generous and good and loving and demonstrative of the life of the Spirit is enormous. But the number of those people who were different from us was very small.

We are to be light and salt in the world, in this whole world, and the light we can give each other whenever we who claim the Holiest of names gather up for worship may well save some of our very souls. Our gathering up in between in the name of fellowship and love and community will do us more good than bad.

But I believe when we go from what we regard as holy places only to provide salt to the ones who are already seasoned, then there will be some places where two or three of God's children who live down the road are gathered, and whose names we do not know, and Jesus may not show up because we who call ourselves by the Holy Name are not there.

I fear we very often miss our chances to be Jesus—to the neighbors we drive past because they are not like us, to the parents of schoolchildren who never come to our homes, to the others in our lives with whom we have far more in common than we know we do, to the ones who want to talk about God but are only willing to hold the conversation over chicken wings and a movie. I often think of us as the ones who are terrified of the storms all around, calling out to our gods, just before we lie down to nap next to Jonah in a comfortable corner of a ship that is breaking up all around us.

The light we Christians bring to each other matters.

But so does the salt that is missing in the world. It may be the only taste in this world some folks ever have of the body of Christ.

To avoid the dark and to pass by the pepper living down the road or down the block or to avoid the sailors who are not like us is to miss a chance for Jesus to turn up wherever two or three are gathered up in the storms or the calms, to avoid the moments where two or three are gathered, and we might be there to see Him or be Him.

Be not afraid.

Be not afraid of the Light that comes from being here among those who bear the Holy Name. Rejoice and be glad of it.

But be not afraid of becoming the salt that seasons the block where you live. Be not afraid of calling upon God on the ships upon which you sail, whoever else may be manning them and wherever they be they headed. Be not afraid of the pepper. This is where we learn to be light and salt in the same way being present to them taught the One Who Came Among Us.

Be not afraid of the publicans and the sinners. We are all living in the desert looking for the strength to make our journey home. Some of those around us are waiting for us.

Friends of Silence and of the Poor

Whatever you do for the least of these, you do for me.

The Gospel

Grant that we may know
and understand the things we ought to do,
and also the power and grace to accomplish them.

The Prayers of the People

I must divide my time for prayer into two parts.

Charles de Foucauld

*I*need to make one stop, to say hello to a friend," said Father Ed.

It was our last night together, the last night of four nights and five days of being with Father Ed, learning about the contemplative life and exploring our practice, "learning to pray with Jesus" was Father Ed's description. The five of us were headed to dinner—four people on retreat and our spiritual director.

We spent our days doing a series of exercises at his direction, taking apart our days and weeks and lives, looking at the way we spend them and the ways we spend time with the One Who Came. At the end of the day, we would make the Eucharist together, and then we would share a simple supper. The evenings were for conversation and reading and walking around the small lake a few yards from our door. This evening, the last evening, we were going to celebrate our time together by going out to dinner. The reservation was made, the departure time was set, and we piled into the car and headed into the Florida sunset.

"It should not take too long to run by. I don't think we have to go too far out of the way," he said as he handed the address to the one of us who was driving. He was not exactly right.

Logistics were never in Father Ed's wheelhouse.

He called me once to tell me he was conducting a workshop close to me and would love to see me. "It is in Murfreesboro," he said, naming a town about forty minutes away from my house. "At the Episcopal Church on Saturday morning at nine." At the appointed hour, I arrived in Murfreesboro. A poster on the door told me the workshop was not in Murfreesboro but in Nashville on Murfreesboro Road, only ten minutes from my house. I missed the session, but I did get to invest three hours for a ten-minute visit before I dropped him at the airport.

Not the first time my director's instructions to me were cryptic. Not the first time his *directee* did not ask enough questions or listen closely either.

Father Ed called me once from Detroit. Detroit was his home, and he taught at a seminary there.

"Robert, I'm flying into Nashville in a few days and I was wondering if I could get a ride from the airport," he said.

"Of course," I said, pleased he would think of me, pleased he would ask a favor of me, pleased I would get to spend a few minutes with him. He often came to Nashville, since he was on the board of a couple spiritual formation organizations in the circles in which I travel. I was happy to take a few minutes from my day and give him a lift.

"Where to?" I said, figuring I would be taking him downtown.

"Oh good," he said, "I am going to Sumatanga," naming the place where he and I had met years before, the place where my spiritual journey had taken a serious turn, a turn that to no small degree was Father Ed's doing. My life's work was waiting there in those woods in northern Alabama, and he helped me to discover it.

Did I mention Father Ed was calling about a lift from the airport to a mountain retreat ground four hours away? Once I said yes, I could not say no. I shifted my calendar around and prepared to head south for a long conversation with the closest thing to a spiritual director I have ever had.

I pulled up outside the airport, and there he was. Classic Irish priest, silver hair and beard, black slacks, black shoes, short-sleeved shirt most likely from Goodwill and worn untucked, a black briefcase in his hand. In the twenty-odd years I saw him travel, he never traveled with a suitcase, only the black, hard-shell briefcase. Alaska, India, Rome, Ireland—no matter where. It did not matter whether he was traveling for three days or three weeks or three months. "Have shirt, have sink, have Woolite, will travel"—the motto of the modern guru.

I had the top down on my little car and he clambered in, saying hello and calling me by the name no one else has ever used for me. No one else has even heard the name, for that matter. It is a secret name, a holy name, a name I heard myself called by the Holy once, and almost never say aloud. Inexplicably, Father Ed ignored my name badge and called me by that name the first time he and I met, many years ago. "I have been waiting for you," he said that day.

He barely spoke to me the whole way down into northern Alabama, he sat guru-like in the sun and the cool spring breeze.

"How lovely," he said when we pulled into the drive two hundred miles away. "I hope we can do this again sometime." He hugged me and gave me a blessing and walked into the lobby of the retreat center, leaving me wondering how he would get home at the end of the week.

And wondering who was going to get him from Rome to Dublin next month.

That evening in Orlando, after a long hour winding and wandering around town, we pulled into the parking lot of a nursing home. As we all piled out, a call was made to change the dinner reservation while Father Ed went to the desk and spoke to the young woman there.

In a minute he came back. "Come on," he said, "let's all go see Joe." We figured he was about to show off his most promising students to one of his old priest friends. He walked in the room and introduced himself to a young man, a young man who was clearly too young for a nursing home to be his home. Father Ed introduced himself and then all of us. We stood at the back of the room, uncomfortable and embarrassed and uncertain. The young man smiled.

Father Ed and Joe had a quiet conversation. Then Father Ed prayed with him and turned to us. "You should get to know Joe," he said over his shoulder as he left the room. Turns out Joe had no idea who Father Ed was, never saw him before in his life.

We followed Ed from room to room for a while. It was strange, walking through these rooms full of strangers, talking to them about their illnesses and their struggles and their hopes and their prayers. Okay, the experience was beyond strange. Uncomfortable is a word that comes to mind.

We returned to the car to head off to our big dinner to celebrate our arrival into the world of contemplative wisdom. No one said anything until we were out of the parking lot.

Father Ed spoke quietly to the windshield in front of him. "If you are going to spend an hour with Jesus in contemplation and prayer and silence and consolation, then you must spend an hour with Jesus who lives in the poor and the sick and the lost and the hungry. Otherwise, you have not really met Him at all."

Passing on the expensive meal, we went for a round of chili dogs and tater tots at the next Sonic we came across, and headed home, very quietly.

The silence continued for a while.

"Whatever you do for the least of these, you do for me," He tells the ones who would follow Him. We smile at their inability to understand the things Jesus told them.

Is our hearing any better, I wonder?

I worry that my practice for prayer—the silence, the reading, the liturgy, the conversation I carry on with Jesus—hunkers me so far down in my relationship with the One Who Came, I miss seeing Him somehow. I worry that I will only see Him in the words that move me, in the answers or lack of them to the petitions and intercessions I make, in the sense of His presence or the lack thereof in the moments when I am in prayer. I have a tendency to go out the door of the places where I pray and only recognize Him as my own life seems touched or untouched by His presence.

I leave the silence and stillness of my practice and often do not notice Him at all until the next time we are alone together and I sit in my oratory and light my candles and ring my bells and make my prayers.

Father Ed was trying to teach me to sit on the steps in front of my house and watch the parade passing by in the little neighborhood where we live as often as I sit in the studio behind my house and make my prayers. He wanted me to learn to be watchful for the Word made flesh as well as the word scribbled on the page, to go out of my way to practice the works of mercy the One Who Came evidently came to show us.

According to the Church, the works of mercy are the things we can do which directly reflect the words Jesus spoke to His disciples and therefore to you and me: Feed the hungry. Give drink to the thirsty. Clothe the naked. Shelter the homeless. Visit the sick. Visit the imprisoned. Instruct the ignorant. Counsel the doubtful. Admonish sinners. Bear wrongs patiently. Forgive offense willingly. Comfort the afflicted. Pray for the living and the dead.

The fact that I may or may not live and breathe and have my being in a part of the one Catholic and Apostolic church that never mentions our responsibility to find Jesus in the hungry and afraid and naked and imprisoned and sick does not excuse me when I pay less attention to the Jesus who needs a cup of cold water even as I pay faithful attention to the Jesus who offers me consolation. I am responsible for offering works of mercy to those in need in my time, in my life, and with my gifts.

A total devotion to only half of Jesus hardly makes for a whole relationship with the One Who Came.

I cannot say for a fact we punched any holes in anyone's darkness on the evening with Father Ed in Orlando, though having spent many days in such places since then, I suspect we did. There were certainly some holes punched in our own darkness. The people we met were still sick and needy after we left. And so were we.

But perhaps some of us even saw Jesus and saw Him well enough to recognize Him when we next see Him. Perhaps we even began to learn to divide our prayer into two parts and make it whole.

Not So Faceless

This is how they know that you love me.

The Gospel

Accept our repentance for our indifference.

Prayers of the People

There is now, living in New York City,
a church-sanctioned hermit, Theresa Mancuso, who wrote recently,
"The thing we desperately need is to face the way it is."

Annie Dillard

*H*ello, Miss Peggy."

One or two days each week in the last few years before she passed away, my mother and I would pull up alongside a battered lawn chair at the stoplight round the corner from the assisted living home where my mother had an apartment. I would roll down the window, and the woman sitting in the lawn chair would come to the car. "You are looking fine today, Miss Peggy," she would say to my mother.

"I am so happy to see you," my mother would answer with the grin she used to charm everyone who ever knew her.

The woman's name is Patricia. She is one of the hundreds of people who sells a newspaper called *The Contributor* on street corners in our town. Like most of them, she has lived a hard life, some by circumstance, some by choice, some by chance. If you hang around *Contributor* folks long enough, you hear story after story of lives lived at the very edge of staying alive at all. They have stories of jail time and drug abuse and homeless living and petty theft and constant hunger and a thousand other things far removed from the ways most of us live our lives.

The Contributor folks are out early each day, having been turned from the shelters where they stay at night or wandering forth from the rooms they rent by the day or the week or from off the park benches or out from under the bridges. They make their way to a distribution point downtown where they trade a few dollars for a pile of newspapers to sell on the corner to make enough money to get by for the day. They carry bags of papers as they take the bus or walk the miles to their assigned or claimed corner where they try to sell papers to the people who pass by in their cars. They have credentials around their neck identifying them as authorized sellers of the paper. The majority of folks who drive past them do not really even see them.

Patricia's corner was outside the place my mother lived after her dementia had become so powerful she needed care around the clock. I would go to pick up my mother to take her to lunch or to the doctor, and her face would light up when she saw Patricia at the corner. I do not think my mother ever remembered her name, but seeing her would always make her happy.

After a while, if you pay attention as you make your rounds of the city, you see the same faces and learn some of their names and some of their stories. You begin to miss them when they are not there, and next thing you know you worry about them.

Demetrious works at the intersection of two main thoroughfares in our city in a part of town where the people who drive by are generally more than a little well-off. When you wave to him, whether you buy a paper or not, you always get a big grin, and always a peace sign.

If you do buy from him, he always autographs his papers and leaves his cell number with you, in case you have an emergency and need a copy of the paper in the middle of the night, I suppose. Demetrious has a teenage son who lives in Birmingham with his mother, and if you catch the stoplight just right, he has time to tell you about his latest bus trip down to see his son play ball.

Jane's post is next to the doorway of the little neighborhood grocery near where I live. A significant portion of the clientele for the store is older ladies who have lived nearby for years, calling the neighborhood their home long before the rest of us came along to help renew the urban, wanting to make our home closer to the heart of the city, driving up the real estate prices and putting up houses and apartment buildings that dwarf their little bungalows. The ladies all know Jane by name and she knows their names too. They buy her papers and she helps them get their groceries in the car.

Her shyness is heartbreaking. It is not hard to believe that without the newspapers to sell she might never have a conversation with anyone anywhere, and certainly not a stranger.

I met Peter one morning while I was sitting at a stoplight on my way downtown to a café where I scribble some days. He held up his paper and made eye contact with me. I held up my copy of this week's paper, and he smiled. I rolled my window down and told him I already bought papers from Demetrious and Jane and Patricia this week, and they would kill me if they knew I was buying from someone else.

He grinned. "You know Patricia?" he asked.

"Sure do."

"Patricia is good people," he said. "Tell her Peter says hey."

There are at least two good things, two bits of light, in all this.

The first is that *The Contributor* folks are being seen. Far too often, the people whose lives cannot be described without using words like broke, homeless, addicted, lost, poor, unfortunate are never seen by those of us for whom the words are merely words read in newspapers or said in our prayers. Far too often, we who live our lives in the same cities and towns never see these folks enough to know their names and their stories. Some of us do indeed man the rooms at Room in the Inn, hand out food bank supplies door-to-door, serve soup in kitchens, teach people to read, and on and on, but not nearly as many of us as one might expect or hope. (Listen carefully—my admiration for those among us who do this work or pay for this work to be done is immense. Let no single one of them believe I am unaware of or downplaying their work for those the rest of us call the least among us.)

But far too many of us—including this particular poet, I am afraid—make out our checks and make our prayers and make up grocery bags of peanut butter and canned goods and make our way to Goodwill to drop off old stuff we no longer want so we can make room for the new stuff we think we need but never know the names or stories of the ones for whom we drop off the envelope in the mailbox, the bag in the narthex, or the trunk load at the dock.

One of the good things about *The Contributor* is that people who are often unseen are now more visible.

The other good thing is that we who would rather not see them are having a harder time ignoring them. Though there are still people in my town who would rather not see them.

In one of our suburbs, there was a great campaign to ensure the folks who sold *The Contributor* could not stand on the street corners and sell the newspaper. The city fathers and mothers decided exposure to the traffic was too dangerous for them and tried to outlaw the practice. The street corners were still safe enough for children on the local high school teams to stand with signs to promote the car wash financing their sporting events and band trips but evidently far too dangerous for grownups trying to make a living selling newspapers.

Could it be we do not want to see "those people," the ones in whom we might see the Christ who is naked and hungry and afraid? Who among us wants to look Christ in the eye through power windows at a stoplight on the way to the mall?

I had a conversation with a pastor of a local church once about these things. Okay, I confess, we managed to escalate from conversation to heated conversation in a relatively short period of time. There is no doubt the whole argument was my fault.

We were talking about the ones among us who have less of everything, about the homeless, the immigrants, all those who live on the margins of the comfortable life both he and I live. With far more sarcasm and self-righteousness in my voice than can ever be justified, I muttered, "Well, when did we see you naked and hungry and afraid?"

He replied with the same degree of self-righteousness, "Don't you go playing the gospel card on me. That's not fair."

As I got out of his car and slammed the door—kind and gentle peacemaker that I clearly am—I began to wonder. If we are not going to pull the gospel card on the ones who claim to believe in the gospel, then why even bother believing in the gospel at all? I should be allowed to pull the card on myself, at the very least.

For a while, the three of us, Peggy and Patricia and I, kept punching holes in each other's darkness, making way for a little bit of the Light of the world to shine through.

"Good morning, Miss Peggy," Patricia would drawl in her two-pack-a-day voice. They would talk, I would pass money for a paper across, the light would change. As we rolled away, my mother and Patricia would exchange waves as I made the turn left onto the road. Miss Peggy would say, "What a sweet girl she is."

After lunch or the doctor visit, I would drop my mother off, and I would circle round to Patricia's corner. "How is Miss Peggy doing now, this day?" Patricia would ask.

I would tell Patricia the reality of it, and she would say she would pray for Peggy and for me. We would both cry and the light would change and I would roll away. Patricia always *saw* Miss Peggy, and she always saw me.

"When did we see *you?*" the disciples asked the Master.

Evidently seeing someone matters, evidently seeing others who are truly *other* is one of the things that suggests to people that I love Him. I cannot be the Christ *to* someone if I do not first see the Christ *in* someone. I can claim status as a follower of the One Who Came, I can write checks, I can drop off canned goods, I can unload my closet, I can say my prayers. But I cannot know the Christ until I see the Christ, not until I look into that face.

12South Film Festival

I have called you friends.

The Gospel

*We entrust all who are dear to us
to your never-failing love and care,
knowing that you will do for them
far more than we can desire or pray for.*

Prayers of the People

*Bad religion has always favored escape, passivity, irresponsibility.
By dint of fixing one's eyes on heaven above,
one does not see what takes place on earth below.*

Father Louis Evely

I got an e-mail a few weeks ago from an old friend.

He is an old friend I have known since my days at the other end of this great long pew known as the Church. He was writing to invite me to come to speak to his evangelical men's group. He thought I might share my thoughts about spiritual friendship between men.

Before I called him back to accept his invitation, I lay down on the floor and laughed out loud. I was not laughing at him or his group, I was laughing at me.

I consider myself qualified to talk to people about people because I confess to liking a couple of dozen or so of them. I am a people person; I just tend to like them in the abstract and generally am happier when none of them are around.

And my years of traveling up and down this great long pew has made of me a confirmed contemplative and sacramentalist, one who likes silence more than songs, sacraments more than sermons, meditation far more than men's groups.

Anyone who has taken the Meyers-Briggs personality profile knows a score of ten to twelve on the introvert scale is a clear indication one is an introvert. My score is twelve to the third power. Wherever two or three are gathered I get a little nervous—especially if they are all men. I maintain a "you guys go have fun hunting or fishing or bowling or playing touch football, whatever you guys do, you can count on me to sit here on the porch guarding your womenfolk" posture at all times.

Most of my relationships, especially with men, have revolved around church or business or sports teams either I or my kids played on. "Robert is my friend," someone might say for no reason other than we attended the same Sunday school class once or negotiated a contract successfully or became simultaneously semi disabled together sitting on bleachers for twelve hours on a hundred Saturdays waiting to catch a glimpse of the eight to twelve minutes each day our kid happened to be on the wrestling mat or in the batter's box.

There is risk associated with being friends with someone, especially if I think there is a chance Jesus has nothing else to do that day and wants to come and be among us. Because if He chooses to be among us, I will only know it if and when I have to look Him in the eye or am forced to muster the courage to try and be the Christ revealed in the room that particular day.

"The secret is this," said Paul, "Christ is in you." Here is another secret: Christ is in the other guy as well.

We love this part, do we not, we who call ourselves by the Holy Name.

We love this part when we look in the mirror. We are less excited about this part when Christ is in someone other, someone genuinely other, and now we have to meet His gaze—your gaze, perhaps—and bind His wounds, put a shirt *and* a cloak on Him, forgive Him over and over and over and over, and be willing to die with Him, if not for Him, even if He may not even notice.

Most days, most all of the days of my life, in fact, I would much rather be left alone.

A year or so ago, I inexplicably made the third or fourth dumbest move I have ever made.

The sweet woman kind enough to marry me was one of the founding members of a women's book club in our neighborhood. The book club was named in honor of another founding member who happened to be a size two.

"You look fabulous," one of the not-exactly-sized-two of them would say to Colleen who owned the neighborhood restaurant where we all met each other, the Colleen who always did indeed look fabulous whenever we were there.

"We hate you for it, too," another one or two would mutter under their breath, just loud enough for everyone to hear.

"You are just bitter," Colleen would say.

Hence, The Bitter Friends of Colleen DeGregory had its first meetings on the banquette in her restaurant. The fabulous Colleen moved away some years ago. She and her good-looking husband spent a year running a restaurant on an island off the coast of Mexico and now they are in New York. Their pictures turn up in *The New York Times* from time to time. Some of us are bitter about that too.

The Bitter Friends now rotate their monthly meetings from house to house, taking turns being the hostess. Once or twice a year, the ladies of the club invite their spouses for Christmas or a cookout. I believe that they believe their spouses apparently do not have a social life. It also may be true they are reluctant to not be in complete control of what little social life we do have. Invariably, the men end up sitting around talking and telling stories and trying to get away with the biggest lie and seeing who can land the biggest laugh.

One Christmas I said to no one in particular, "We guys should start a movie club. We could meet on the Monday the week after the ladies have had their book club meeting. I mean, the house will already be clean."

Someone heard me evidently, thus establishing the Rule of the 12South Film Festival. Not exactly the Rule of St. Benedict, but community has to start somewhere. If not the first, it was one of the few times in my life I achieved what one might call consensus. And I have been paying the price for it ever since.

The 12South Film Festival is an exclusive group. No one can join unless his spouse or partner is a member of The Bitter Friends. We cannot even choose who will have a social life with or without their approval. We can only add a new member if they do first.

Our name is known in the neighborhood now, mostly because we are founding sponsors of the Sevier Park Concert Series, held annually in the park down the way. Our name is on the T-shirt, and on the banner above the stage, and we are grandfathered in to all the after-parties, which is the actual reason we pooled our money and bought space on the banner in the first place.

People call the neighborhood association and ask questions. "We have our own film festival?" "Can I join?" "How can I be in touch with them?" "Who are they?"

We coached the association director to reply, "We know who they are. We cannot tell you their names. We will tell them you inquired."

None of the film club members are very much like the others at all.

Between us all we can boast of a lawyer, two war veterans, an ophthalmologist, an assistant dean at a university, a film director, a church musician at a small church, two civil servants, an architect, a poet, and two people who travel and speak. We are Episcopalian, agnostic, atheist, Catholic, evangelical Christian, Presbyterian, and noncombatant.

One of us does very sophisticated IT work for national law firms for a living, and another is a tireless advocate for liberal causes and the unofficial mayor of our neighborhood. One gave up a promising career with big eyeglass stores in the mall to work at a veterans hospital, and another goes to Mass every day. One makes films, and another has spent the last three years caring for his dying parents. One is still so defeated by the toxic nature of the church he grew up in he will not darken the door of one whereas another of us has done nearly everything in the name of Christian worship save handling snakes and visiting the Vatican.

Between the eight of us we have fought in three wars, married more than a dozen times, fathered almost twenty children, own a fishing boat, and sport an average golf handicap of roughly fifty-one. When our turn comes to host the Film Festival, we can cook steaks, spaghetti and meatballs, vegetarian, warmed-over barbecue from the place down the street, a serious crawfish boil, big time chicken wings, whatever is the special at a nearby white tablecloth restaurant, and the best Bolognese sauce in this town.

One or more of us is hard to get along with when he has had too much to drink. Another cannot explain his political positions even to those of us inclined to agree with him. One of us pulls away whenever the conversation gets too close to the bone, and another is so anxious to please he will say nearly anything. One of us is so desperate to be taken seriously he overstates everything, and another is so shy we are all still trying to get a real sense of him. One has a habit of asking another question before you can answer the last one while another Googles the answer to every question asked of everyone before any of us have a chance to rack our brains to come up with the answer. (What is the use of having a brain if you are not going to rack the thing every once in a while?)

As a group, we are as smart as a whip and as dumb as dirt, as loose as a goose, as wound too tight, as oblivious and as attentive, as devoted to the things we believe in and as intolerant of folks who believe otherwise, and as generous and as exasperating as any crowd of folks I have ever known, including every crowd of every kind of Christians I have ever frequented as I have made my way up and down this great long pew we call the Church.

But I also have to say this: These people never pretend. They never let you get away with clichés. They never go out of their way to tell you how great their lives are going when they are not. They never hold back. When the storms come, they pray to their gods and then come and help you throw things overboard and clean up the mess and make it to shore.

They always give you a big hug or a big shout whenever they greet you and whenever they are headed home, even though at least two of us want to choke at least two of the rest of us on the way out the door.

Having friends is a new experience for me, and I am still not completely convinced it is a good idea.

For starters, if you have friends, they interrupt you and want you to do things—have a coffee, go to the movies, watch their kids for a couple of hours, show up at a neighborhood event and hand out flyers. They like for you to set up chairs for their kid's wedding in the park while they are at the champagne party for the groom, and you are not invited precisely because you are setting up chairs in the park for the wedding. They want you to crawl out of bed early on Saturday morning to cheer their wife on while she comes in two places from dead last in the local fun run. (There is no such thing as a fun run, by the way, no matter what anyone pretends. Watching a fun run is no fun either.)

They will call you on the weekends, knock on your door, expect you to come to dinner when they invite you, expect you to invite them to dinner simply because you ate at their house once. Then there is the texting. And the waking you up in the middle of some storm in the night to check on you while you were sleeping peacefully through all of Mother Nature's ruckus.

Evidently, old dogs can learn new tricks, but in my experience, an old dog can pull a muscle very easily. I have had to learn several new tricks since I wandered into the world of actual friendship.

I am learning that any fool can be a friend to people like themselves, it takes something deeper to be a friend to people who are different. It takes something like whatever was in Jesus that caused Him to choose publicans and sinners over religious folks.

Maybe He was being a physician to those in need, as the Gospels tell us He said. Maybe He was just tired of the same old pious conversations with the same folks who were living the same life He was living, and He wanted to add a little more spice to the life to which He was being drawn.

Almost every meeting of the Film Festival includes twenty to thirty minutes of intense theological discussion—no matter what the film is. Everything we watch leads to a discussion of the glimpses of the Holy to be found outside the realm of the holy spaces some of us attend to and about what those glimpses of the Holy might mean in our lives. The ones who lead the conversation that way are never the Christians.

The ones who lead the conversation that way are the atheists and the agnostics. Their language is different than mine, but their questions are the ones I have asked my entire life.

In fact, there is a running joke in the group about my not being allowed to talk during this part of the discussions. On the first occasion, my wise spiritual self kept trying to get a word in edgewise, but I was talked over by some louder person at the table. I am shy enough to keep backing off. After about forty minutes, one of the guys said, "I suppose we could ask the writer of religious books what he thinks about this religious stuff."

Before I could offer what would have been very wise insight, one of my friends yelled out, with a grin on his face, "No, no, no, keep him quiet. I have already made up my mind." I laughed louder than anyone, or at least I hope I did. I meant to laugh.

There I was, renowned wise, spiritual teacher, recognized as qualified light and salt in the world, reduced to listening as the pepper would not pipe down long enough for me to season him properly.

Ever since, when the conversation turns to religion or spirituality or theology, the same guy will always say, "It's Robert's turn now. We really should let him talk. Maybe we will learn something." He always says it with the same big grin on his face. He has taught me to grin back.

He also still claims atheist credentials, but I have come to see him as an atheist who wants to talk about the meaning of a Presence he professes not to believe in. We both believe in the same God, though only one of the two us has the audacity to say it aloud, and when I do, I whisper it with fear and with trembling every time.

The 12South Film Festival is teaching me this: The big questions are not going unasked by the people who are not going to the places we go to on Sundays and Wednesdays and whenever else we gather up. They are, however, all too often being asked in gatherings we do not attend.

I spent much of my life being sure I was with right crowd of folks and not hanging out with the publicans and the sinners.

The result was I may well have missed a moment or two or ten thousand in which two or three were gathered, and Jesus was not in fact among them or went unseen because I was not among them.

It is just as true I missed more than a few chances to see Him—to see Him imprisoned by fear, a bad marriage, disease, financial worries, some bad habit or another, exhaustion at caring for his family—and all because I wanted to be assured I was hanging out with the right kind of folks.

If you think I am saying that a gathering up of like-minded folks in church settings week after week is somehow wrong, I have been unclear. If you think I believe such gatherings cannot lead to deep and meaningful and powerful moments of opening ourselves up to each other and to the One Who Made Us, then I may not yet poet enough to articulate what the Film Festival is teaching me.

But I am poet enough to say this: The One Who Came Among Us went out of His way to be with the ones who were not like Him. And in the end, He called them His friends.

A Last Thing

I have told you these things that my joy may be in you,
and so that your joy will be complete.

The Gospel

Grant that we find you and be found by you.

The Prayers of the People

We are invited to forget ourselves on purpose,
cast our awful solemnity to the winds
and join in the general dance.

Thomas Merton

A ttending church is not always the reason one travels to Paris. It certainly is not the reason we went, but it may turn out to have been one of the reasons I was there.

We arrived early in the morning, as you often do when you travel to Europe. It was the day before Palm Sunday. In an effort to be faithful Anglicans the next morning, we wandered out early, went to a café, and had a bite of bread—one of the actual reasons one goes to Paris ever and at all. Then we took the Metro up to Avenue Saint George and walked the few blocks to The American Cathedral.

The Cathedral itself is beautiful, as one would expect of an Anglican house of worship built one hundred and twenty-five years ago in a spot a few blocks from the Seine and a few blocks from the *Arc de*

Triomphe. The beauty and the quiet and the peace of the great cathedral was enough to make us smile a grateful smile.

In Paris, one can find a sacred room to do that to you every few blocks. What made this different, at least for us, was the way the people there were carrying on. Their joy overwhelmed us.

The acolytes grinned as they led the processional, actual teenagers wearing robes and proper shoes and carrying crosses and smiling anyway. The choir passed us singing for all they were worth, as though they even believed some of what they were singing. Watching them, watching their heads move with the great hymns of the day as they took their places in the choir made us want to sing for all we were worth too.

The readers read thoughtfully, the dean sermonized intelligently, and the bishop greeted us with warmth and humor. The ushers who guided us up the stairs to the altar to make the Eucharist smiled and nodded to everyone as though they had known all of us all their lives.

It was a joy with its roots in something other than programs or postures or pretense or presumption. It seemed a deep and rich joy, a joy growing of good tidings of great joy. That is, after all, the reason to even build such a building and muster up such a gathering.

A long stretch of time had passed since we had been in a cathedral. We were more hungry for it than we knew. We were happy to follow Merton's advice.

There was nothing for us to do but join in, which we proceeded to do two or three times each week for the whole time we were in Paris. There was as much joy on the faces of the parishioners at morning prayer as there was on the festival day we attended when we first arrived.

Perhaps churches everywhere are that way all of the time and I have just been hanging around the wrong folks. Perhaps I am too tired and worn by the time I enter a sanctuary and am incapable of recognizing the deep joy before me. Perhaps I have been going for the wrong reasons—"for solace and not for strength," as the ancient prayer admonishes.

Or perhaps all too often we church folks inadvertently create our own bushels out of programs and rules and stewardship drives and the things of this world, bushels that hide the Light of the world from those who need it most, including our own sweet selves.

I believe we are to spend our days and hours, our love and our work, our presence and our hopes punching holes in the darkness rather than hunkering down and trying to protect ourselves from the darkness that seems all around us.

Where there is Light, we are to celebrate. Where there is darkness, we are to raise our fist and punch a hole in it—as hard as we can, as often as we can. The size of the hole does not matter, the fact of it is what counts more than everything.

Evidently, that is how the Light of the world sneaks in. And precisely how our joy—the joy of the One Who Came Among Us—has been, is now, and ever will be made complete.

A Few Notes, if I May

About the Word *Kingdom*

Some folks have a great deal of difficulty with the use of the word *kingdom* to describe the way of God being among us and coming to us. I am among those who wish there was a better word, a word that would not be hard for *all* of us to hear. The difficulty for this writer is that the other words one might use—*reign of God*, for example—are no more expressive and far less poetic than the one I have fallen back on. I looked at French words, Italian words, bend-over-backward English phrases, and finally made an honest choice based on my poet's ear.

My hope is the rest of the language I have used here will demonstrate I am aware of such difficulties and I am learning. If I am not moving fast enough, I beg forgiveness and pledge to keep trying.

About the Epigraphs and the Quotations

The scriptures in the epigraphs are from John, the Gospel and the Letters. The paraphrasing is mine. Scripture is alive, living and breathing. Looking at the forty or fifty translations and paraphrases I have on my shelves, I have come to believe even I cannot hurt the Story of Us All. Neither can you; feel free to make it your own.

The prayers are adapted from the contemporary—what a cute word—version of *The Book of Common Prayer*, 1979. Though I have noted them as from *The Prayers of the People*, they are not all strictly such. I chose them from several places in Father Cranmer's masterpiece of liturgical practice. The whole book could be called the prayers of the people as far as I am concerned.

The other voices are from a crowd of poets and pundits and pilgrims who have worked to try and make a writer of me for years. The following is a list in the order in which they appear. Thank you to them all for what their words have meant to me. Poets and pilgrims of one sort or another, I recommend them to you and encourage you to find and live under the influence of their work.

Fr. Thomas Cranmer	*Thomas Merton*
Leonard Cohen	*Joseph Campbell*
St. Frances of Assisi	*Fr. Henri Nouwen*
Mary Oliver	*Reuben Welch*
Jackson Browne	*Fr. Charles de Foucauld*
Ralph Keyes	*Fr. Edward Farrell*

Frederick Buechner   *Annie Dillard*

Fr. John Dominic Crossan   *Fr. Louis Evely*

About Several Folks Who Make My Work Possible

Among them are the fine folks at Abingdon—past and present. Some of them became and remain particular friends of mine over the years, and others of them are becoming so. All of them are kind enough to make room for my voice—especially Susan and Ramona and Tamara and Sonua, and now Deanna and Brenda and Dawn and Susan the Patient.

As always, I am grateful to Miss Jones of Merigold who has cleared the way for me all along the way.

Lastly, I Shall Invoke Ms. Tickle's Name Again

There are now only stories of her, no Tickle to talk to, to visit, to come across at a book show. Many hearts always will be full of the memory of you, and empty at the absence of you.

You brought to us and left with us a certain and immense joy—a joy rooted in the love of the Holy and the love of the Word and the love of our art. That joy will always remain, and no one will take that joy from us.

Thanks be to Ms. Tickle. Thanks be to God. Thanks be.

Namasté.

R. Benson
Brightwood, 2016

References

Browne, Jackson, and Bryan Garofalo, "The Load-Out" (New York: Elektra / Asylum Records, 1977).

Buechner, Frederick, *Now and Then* (San Francisco: HarperSanFrancisco, 1983).

Campbell, Joseph, *The Power of Myth* (New York: Anchor, 1988).

Cohen, Leonard, "Anthem" (Stranger Music, 1992).

Dillard, Annie, *For the Time Being* (New York: Vintage, 2000).

Grimes, William, "Clive Barnes, Who Raised Stakes in Dance and Theater Criticism, Dies at 81," NYTimes online, Nov. 19, 2008. www.nytimes.com/2008/11/20/arts/dance/20barnes.html?_r=0.

Merton, Thomas, "The General Dance," in *Thomas Merton, Spiritual Master: The Essential Writings*, ed. Lawrence Cunningham (Mahwah, NJ: Paulist, 1992).

Merton, Thomas, *Run to the Mountain: The Story of a Vocation, The Journal of Thomas Merton*, vol. 1: 1939–1941 (New York: HarperOne, 1996).

Nouwen, Henri, *The Wounded Healer: Ministry in Contemporary Society* (New York: Doubleday, 1972).

Oliver, Mary, "When Death Comes," in *New and Selected Poems*, vol. 1 (Boston: Beacon, 1992).

About the Author

Robert Benson has written more than twenty books about the search for and the discovery of the Holy in the midst of our everyday lives, work critically acclaimed in publications as diverse as *The New York Times*, *Publishers' Weekly*, and *American Benedictine Review*.

He is a lifelong churchman, an alumnus of The Academy for Spiritual Formation, a member of The Friends of Silence & of the Poor, and was named a Living Spiritual Teacher by Spirituality & Practice.com. He travels the country speaking for a wide variety of retreats and conferences.

He lives and writes, pays attention and says his prayers at his home in Nashville, Tennessee. He is always happy to hear from folks at Post Office Box 121994, Nashville 37212 or at rbstudio2@mac.com.

Also by Robert Benson

Between the Dreaming and the Coming True
Living Prayer
Venite: A Book of Daily Prayer
The Night of the Child
The Game: One Man, Nine Innings, A Love Affair with Baseball
That We May Perfectly Love Thee
The Body Broken
A Good Life
Home by Another Way
Daily Prayer: A Little Book for Saying the Daily Office
Digging In: Tending to Life in Your Own Backyard
In Constant Prayer
The Echo Within
A Good Neighbor
Moving Miss Peggy
Dancing on the Head of a Pen
Notes From Home*
(*e-book only from Amazon)

Continued from front

"Benson challenges each of us to reexamine what it means to be a follower of Jesus in the diverse body of Christ." —**Dave Burchett**, author of *Bring 'Em Back Alive* and *When Bad Christians Happen to Good People*

"In this so-beautiful book, Robert Benson provides the sky in which your soul can soar. You can fly." —**Leonard Sweet**, author of *The Gospel According to Starbucks*

"Robert Benson reminds us of what we too often forget—that the ground we walk upon is sacred." —**Frederic and Mary Ann Brussat**, coauthors of *Spiritual Literacy* and directors of SpiritualityandPractice.com

"Again and again, Robert Benson speaks to my heart." —**Luci Shaw**, writer-in-residence, Regent College, and author of *Water Lines*

"As always, Benson's deceptively simple storytelling sneaks up on you. His style—a fusion of gentleness, raw truth, and quiet power (remind you of anyone?)—is put to good use." —**Nikki Grimes**, award-winning author

"Robert Benson has a lyrical style that winds itself around your heart, then lowers the boom with a heavy dose of realism." —**Carol Holquist**, editor

Praise from Media for Robert Benson's Works

"It is a personal essay of sorts, the kind which is a joy to read…so personal that the reader will feel he knows Robert Benson as an old friend. It is disappointing to awaken from the text and realize otherwise." —**BookPage**

"Benson's tone remains chatty and down-to-earth, and the analogies he draws hit the mark." —**The New York Times Book Review**

"…charming and elegantly written….That rare gift, a thought-provoking record of his own spiritual quest for God through the dark night of depression….Willa Cather's phrase, 'Thy will be done in art as it is in heaven' could serve as an epigraph to this fine work." —**Publishers Weekly**

"The author's language is graceful and his ideas graced." —**American Benedictine Review**

"...a refreshingly candid, funny and deeply serious look at his life and how the mystery of prayer came to be a part of it." —**Knoxville News-Sentinel**

"In his use of traditions and time-honored mentors ranging from Church fathers and mystics of Jewish and eastern persuasions, he sows broadly and deeply, making this book a universal read." —**Praying**

"One does not read an account such as Benson's to get a theology lesson as much as to stand alongside someone who is listening to God. Reading becomes a kind of sanctified eavesdropping, standing by a cracked-open chapel door to overhear what God tells Benson so we, too, can hear the Voice we long to hear. Because of Benson's courage and honesty, we hear and learn." —**Weavings: A Journal of the Christian Spiritual Life**